P9-DEG-252

Karl Rahner

KARL RAHNER

An Introduction to His Theology

KARL-HEINZ WEGER

A CROSSROAD BOOK · THE SEABURY PRESS · NEW YORK

1980
The Seabury Press
815 Second Avenue · New York, N.Y. 10017

Published originally as *Karl Rahner: Eine Einführung in sein theologisches Denken.* Copyright © 1978 Verlag Herder, Freiburg im Breisgau, Federal Republic of Germany

Translated from the German by David Smith. English translation Copyright © 1980 Search Press Limited. All rights reserved.
No part of this book may be reproduced, stored in a retrieval system, or transmitted, in any form or by any means, electronic, mechanical, photocopying, recording, or otherwise, without the written permission of The Seabury Press.
Printed in the United States of America

Library of Congress Cataloging in Publication Data
Weger, Karl-Heinz.
Karl Rahner, an introduction to his theology.
Translation of Karl Rahner, Eine Einführung in sein theologisches Denken.
"A Crossroad book."
Bibliography
1. Rahner, Karl, 1904-   I. Title
BX4705.R287W4313   230'.2'0924   79–27424
ISBN 0–8164–0127–6

Contents

Foreword

Heinz-Joachim Fischer, discussing Karl Rahner in a newspaper article, said of his work: 'Rahner was a breath of fresh air for anyone studying Catholic theology in the nineteen-sixties. Most students thought of Catholic dogmatic theology in particular as a Procrustean bed, in which nonacceptable ideas were simply lopped off. But it was possible to breathe freely in the atmosphere created by Rahner. Equipped with the conviction of his own powerful ideas, he plunged through the tangled thicket of incomprehensible formulae, cut through apparent problems and cleared the way for long-forgotten Christian doctrines to be seen again'.[1] Many people had this experience of Rahner in the nineteen-sixties and are still experiencing his theology as a way to faith.

Nevertheless, it is becoming increasingly difficult to approach Rahner's work, especially for those who are embarking for the first time on a study of his theology and for those who are not professional theologians. He has written an immense number of articles and books, all in a distinctive terminology and based on a specific method, and this alone calls for a great effort on the part of the reader. Many prospective readers do not feel equal to the task.

It is simply not possible to present Rahner's theological work in an abbreviated form and in a comprehensive survey at one and the same time. Nor do I attempt to do so in this little book. His work is too wide-ranging and exists at too many different levels. My aim, in this introduction to the theological thought of Karl Rahner, is not to provide a substitute for Rahner himself, a theology that can be read instead of his own work. On the contrary, all that I have tried to do is to write an introductory guide to enable students of Rahner to understand more clearly his concepts, method and, perhaps most important of all, intention.

I would agree with Vorgrimler, who once declared: 'Even in the twenty-first century Catholic theology will still be deeply influenced by Rahner's work.'[2] I believe that this is a true forecast, partly because Rahner himself has said, looking back over his own career: 'I certainly did not become a theologian with the aim of introducing new ideas or of heralding or inaugurating a new period of theology. I am a Jesuit, a member of a religious order and a priest. As a theologian, I had to give lectures. I have been interested in all the things that I have had to do and, broadly speaking, I have given myself body and soul to all of them.'[3] It is true, of course—very little in his life has been due to chance. Body and soul, he has worked ceaselessly to produce a body of theology that eminently merits a careful exposition.

Finally, I feel bound to point out what must be well known to anyone who is familiar with Rahner's writings, namely that any introduction to his theological thought will inevitably be an incomplete and fragmentary simplification. One is certain to make a number of perhaps personal emphases. My intention throughout, however, has been to produce no more than a guide to Rahner's theology[4] and, just as many have been helped by that theology, so too may, I hope, many be helped by this introduction. I hope especially that it will point in the direction from which an answer will come to the question asked by Rahner himself in one of his articles: 'Why am I a Christian today?'[5]

Munich, Summer 1978   *Karl-Heinz Weger*

·1·

From Necessity to Method

German-speaking Catholic theologians were confronted with a completely new situation in the nineteen-fifties. Exegetes had won a certain freedom for themselves, for the most part in contradiction to the literal interpretation of the pronouncements of the Papal Biblical Commission. Pastoral theologians had observed that prosperous middle-class Christians were less interested in religious questions and, according to dogmatic theologians, there was as little satisfaction with the manuals of theology among adults as there was enthusiasm among children for learning the catechism by heart.

Clearly, a change had taken place in attitudes. There was no longer a demand to be taught faith as such. This had been replaced by a desire to understand and particularly to understand the most important aspects of faith. Very soon it became obvious that the bridge between faith and everyday life or religion and reality was too weak to support traffic. It was precisely the most fundamental aspects of faith that modern man found strange and even unintelligible. It seemed, in other words, as though two different worlds were opposed to each other. A gulf had opened up between Christian faith expressed in firm concepts and everyday reality. Faith called for an increasing effort on the part of those who professed it. It had to be given more and more support from outside. It was something that appeared dressed in special clothes on Sunday and had little to do with everyday life. What meaning could concepts such as grace and redemption, the incarnation of God, heaven and hell, original sin, the Trinity, and the Immaculate Conception have for those working at the conveyor belt or in the office? A crisis had arisen in faith which even now has not been fully overcome. Why did it arise? What precisely was no longer in accord with the contemporary situation in what Rahner himself calls 'scholastic theology'? How had it come about that the manuals of dogmatic theology, and the catechism for the children of the 'simple faithful' that had been based on those manuals, said everything and yet, in the end, nothing?

Scholastic theology Not Suitable

There was, then, obviously a crisis of faith and its presentation. Correspondingly, there was a need for Catholic theologians who were both gifted thinkers and able to begin by asking what Metz has called childishly difficult questions and by reflecting in an entirely new way about faith. From this new necessity, a new method had to be found. But what, then, was the basis of this necessity arising from the contemporary crisis in faith?

The Faith-Crisis of a New Generation

Ever since he has become more widely known both to students of theology and to interested lay people—and his fame has been steadily increasing from the nineteen-fifties onwards—Karl Rahner has given three main reasons for the present crisis in faith. Unlike people in the past, we are living now in a pluralistic epoch. This phenomenon is present both inside and outside the Church. We live with an almost unaccountable number of varying convictions. The closed society of the past has become the open society of the present. Rahner himself has pointed out that, in the constant life-and-death struggle of modern secularized

① Pluralism

society, theologians are constantly faced with the ultimate questions of a personal decision for God, Christ, and the Church. They have, as Rahner has always stressed, to find an answer to these questions.

This pluralism is closely connected with—and has to some extent been caused by—modern man's greatly enlarged field of knowledge. Theologians have therefore to take this wider knowledge into account. When he began to study theology before World War II, Rahner was, in his own words, much more knowledgeable than he is now, bearing in mind the extent of knowledge available to a theologian in those times. Now, however, there are so many historical, metaphysical, philosophical, sociological, and religious problems that he confesses that he feels himself to be much more stupid than in the past, confronted with so much material available to the theologian.

This is not an ironical statement. It is rather an admission that he feels himself on the one hand compelled again and again to question the intellectual honesty of faith today and, on the other, to question faith itself and its fundamental tenets, almost as an amateur theologian. He has said publicly that he has always striven to be an amateur theologian in a certain sense, claiming this right in order to be able to cope with the vast number of scientific and specialized problems that present themselves to man today in a non-objective and unmethodical way. This he described as a 'malicious but serious statement'. He went on to stress that he had always tried to be a thoughtful and conscious amateur above all in his approach to the ultimate and fundamental questions of theology as a whole.

One of the most striking aspects of modern man's much wider knowledge is his consciousness of history. It is this historically conscious man who is faced with the Catholic faith of the past. What does this mean? History, it would seem, always deals with contingencies and coincidences.

Napoleon's campaign against Russia, for example, was a historical fact, but it was not a historical necessity. It might have happened differently. Necessity seems to play little part in history, which is characterized by what simply happened to take place.

Strikingly enough, but quite consistently, modern man applies his historical awareness to his faith. One often hears such statements as: That is an article of faith! It is in the Bible! We must believe that, it is the Church's teaching! Such statements are accepted or they are not accepted; an article is believed or it is not believed. As a religion based on God's revelation of himself in human history, Christian faith is marked by the fact that it is 'merely' historical. It did not, in other words, have of necessity to be what it became and now is, if God had wanted it to be different. What it is, however, and has become in history is of absolute importance to man.

Contemporary man's consciousness of history, to which I shall return later in greater detail, is also accompanied by a knowledge of history and man's cultural development, and Rahner is acutely aware of the effect that this has had on man's awareness of faith today. We all know that there are many myths in which an incarnation of God plays a leading part. Rahner invites us to look soberly at the spiritual situation in which man is placed today. If someone who has not been brought up as a Christian hears the statement: 'Jesus is God incarnate', he will probably reject it as mythological. Rahner himself soberly accepts this as a probable fact and then says that we, in the West, would react in the same way if we were to hear for the first time that the Dalai Lama seriously thinks that he is a re-incarnation of the Buddha.

In the light of this contemporary consciousness and knowledge of history, Rahner is opposed to a merely positive knowledge of faith acquired by a process of learning. If the mere fact of the revelation of God's word

were really so absolutely compelling and obvious as we have
been taught to believe, he insists, then the content of it could
be positively imposed as a mystery that need not be
discussed. If, however, Rahner goes on to say, modern man
finds that he cannot believe the content of God's revelation
and if theology is responsible for this, then he will quite
logically feel justified in experiencing even stronger doubts
about the very fact of revelation. It is typical of Rahner's
thinking that he even goes a stage further and declares that
modern man's difficulties can all be traced back to what he
calls a 'formal structure'. By this he means that theological
statements are not expressed in such a way that the content
of those statements is immediately recognizable as being
directly related to a man's interpretation of his own experience. In fact, Rahner has frequently called modern man's
attitude towards faith the result of indoctrination. The
Christian is all too often taught by rote and externally
indoctrinated; consequently, he has little idea of what faith
means for life as a whole.

Pluralism in convictions, both philosophical and religious,
and greatly extended knowledge, comprise one powerful
reason why modern man's faith is in a state of crisis. This
crisis cannot, in Rahner's opinion, be overcome by the
methods of scholastic theology.

A further difficulty that has been present for some time is
the calcification of theological concepts. Rahner has frequently pointed out in his writings that there has been, until
quite recently, a widely-held conviction that there is no more
essential work to be done in the field of theology; that the
history of dogma is at an end; and that the terminology
traditionally used in dogmatic theology cannot be replaced
by new terms and concepts. Hence the results of theological
debate, particularly in the dogmatic sphere, have not been
regarded as open.[6]

Both the proclamation of the Gospel and Christian

worship, Rahner has said, have, until recently, been based to
a greater or lesser extent on the traditional statements made
and the articles of faith formulated during the first fifteen or
so centuries of Christian history. During most of this long
period, Christianity found itself in a more or less homoge-
neous spiritual and intellectual climate, and theology was
able to provide a consistent accompaniment to the melody of
these formulae of faith. Now, however, Rahner hastens to
add, the radically changed situation compels theologians to
make new pronouncements about the content of the same
faith. This, he insists, is their first and most important task.

For Rahner theology has always been a historical study.
This means that his theology is clearly distinguished from
the traditional theology of the Church. He has not hesitated,
for example, to apply Bultmann's highly charged word
'demythologization' to Catholic theology, although he does
not, of course, use the term in exactly the same way as
Bultmann used it; he does not insist that Catholic theologians should demythologize their own theology. In the same
context in which he spoke about this need for theologians to
express the old faith in new concepts, he also pointed
emphatically to the almost completely unsuitable nature of
the traditional statements about faith, at least for the
immediately necessary proclamation of faith.

It is obviously necessary, Rahner believes, but it must also
be possible to know what is meant by the earlier statements
of faith, and to reformulate this content so that it accords
with modern man's understanding of himself and his world.
The new situation in which faith is, for many different
reasons, placed calls for a new language of faith, and this
new language cannot under any circumstances be the ghetto
language of the initiated.

Rahner is convinced of the historical nature of theological
research. The fact that we have certain fundamental concepts in our theological vocabulary does not necessarily

mean, he has said, that they are permanently and immovably fixed in the theological firmament and will shine for ever over the future history of theology. Of course Rahner is not the only theologian to have become intensely conscious of the historical character of theology and of faith itself, but he is perhaps the Catholic theologian who has expressed this conviction most clearly and insistently since the nineteen-fifties. We are caught up in that history, and our faith has consequently to be adapted, without recourse to facile compromise, to the new historical situation in which we find ourselves today.

We have reached a knowledge of what is eternal and true within history, and we can only possess that eternal truth, Rahner maintains, if we entrust ourselves to the further course of history. If we refuse to take that risk, the traditional dogmatic statements quickly become unintelligible and opaque, like shuttered window-panes through which God's light cannot shine. We use the word 'person', he continues, because our thought is almost inevitably historically conditioned—to mean something that we have not been allowed to conceive in considering the dogma of the Trinity or the Church's traditional Christology. This is but one example. Rahner also mentions in this context such terms as 'marriage', 'bread', and 'wine'. Any theologian whose thinking is at all subtle will know what to do in such a case, but what, he asks, can the 'ordinary consumer' of theology make of this? We may conclude, then, with Rahner that we all have to bear the burden of history—all of us, including theologians.

Pluralism, the great extension of man's knowledge in the present century, and the calcification of theological concepts, which have either changed in meaning in the course of history or no longer correspond to changed conditions of life—these are, in Rahner's view, the three most important factors in the present crisis of faith. All three are in one way or another connected with man's historical development. As we have seen, Rahner has always insisted that theologians should take pluralism seriously into account and constantly bear in mind that their work is intended for people whose knowledge is far greater than that of the 'simple faithful' of previous generations. One of his cardinal principles is that the content and the concepts of faith should be open to the future. There should also be no enforced indoctrination of the statements of faith, and what is said about faith should accord with man's present-day understanding of himself and the world.

In view of this, we are bound to question the relationship between revelation and faith. Rahner has repeatedly asked whether it is possible to show, in a given historical situation or personal experience, that anything historical (for example, either the historical Jesus or the history of Christian faith), by which we mean contingencies or coincidences (i.e., what in fact happened, but might have happened either differently or not at all), can be proved to be true. Can an intention be recognized behind faith that is based on a historical event; and can this intention be expressed, without falsifying this historical event, so that it accords with my understanding of myself and the world? Is it possible to learn about what we are taught to believe as Christians in any way that is not based on being instructed by an external authority, or in a way that makes it more than it really is?

In his answers to these questions, Rahner has not followed what might have been the obvious path of Dilthey and his successors, who emphasized the need for a psychological approach to the past, by means of empathy. (It is possible that he was not in fact familiar with this method.) He has also eschewed the well-known question of the historical Jesus as a field that has already been fully explored. Instead he has borrowed from philosophy what he calls the 'transcendental and anthropological method' in theology, and has followed this way so consistently throughout his working life that it has increasingly become the apparatus which dominates his whole thinking.

Because it is of such central importance in his thinking, I shall discuss the structure of this transcendental and anthropological method and its implications for Rahner's theology in greater detail in the following section. Nevertheless, I can say straightaway that it can to some extent be summarized in the formula: faith as experience of myself and with reference to my own life. It has certainly proved possible, by using this method, for Rahner to tackle the problem of the relationship between God's revelation of himself in history and man's experience of himself. Two aspects of this problem stand out as of paramount importance. I shall consider these immediately.

The first has been formulated in the following way by Rahner himself. We cannot, without falling into the heresy of Modernism, try to deduce complete theological statements from man's experience of himself, and treat them as a conceptual objectivization and expression of that experience. This, Rahner stresses, has never been his intention. Even if this question is disregarded, however, it is still possible to think of the connection between human experience and the content of dogmatic statements as something quite different from a simple logical deduction or explicitation. Rahner concludes this definition of the first aspect of the problem with the words: 'there are connections based on analogy'.

The second aspect of the problem of the relationship between historical revelation and human experience was outlined by Rahner in a reply given to a direct question asked by an interviewer. His answer shows that he is fully aware of the difficulty that arises as a result of this relationship: 'I would say that there are very few philosophical, anthropological, or theological problems that are more difficult to solve in a correct and balanced way than that of the relationship between transcendentality and history'.

Critical Problem

If faith and modern man's experience of himself have to be related to each other, and if it is essential to understand not only faith, but its connection with life, and to appreciate the existential significance of faith, a question inevitably arises: how can an historical event, which, as we have seen, is apparently not necessary, but contingent, be of essential importance for man in a particular period of history and have a decisive effect on his life? This question contains the dilemma that confronts any revealed religion based on historical events. This dilemma can be defined in the following way. On the one hand, the unique aspect of the historical event or events and its (or their) significance can be stressed in theology, in which case a statement about faith can soon become 'what simply happened', and therefore have very little to do with man's experience of himself. On the other hand, however, the aspect of man's being that transcends time and history may be emphasized in theology, when history will inevitably become no more than a series of cases, in which nothing really new happens and every historical event is simply an interpretation of the transcendental reality which is authentic, where the historical reality is not. In other words, history soon becomes something of secondary importance in the world. How, then, should it have reached a unique and unrepeatable climax in the particular historical event of Jesus of Nazareth?

This aspect of the problem is something with which modern man is very familiar. It is perhaps the most fundamental reason for the contemporary crisis of faith. How, Rahner has asked, can Jesus do more than simply give us the courage to believe in the love and forgiveness of God that exists but is not brought about by him? Jesus is a good example of courage, and of faith and hope in God, but he had these qualities in a different age and in a world that is alien to us. The problem of the relationship between transcendence and history is acute.

Rahner has, however, attempted to solve this dilemma, which has arisen in the case of every religion based on a historical revelation, in spite of the reservations that I have mentioned. He is intensely aware of the crisis of faith experienced by our generation. We cannot, he knows, list all the reasons for this crisis, but some are clear and beyond dispute and it is worth repeating them briefly.

Modern man is intellectually honest in his attitude towards the pluralism of contemporary philosophical and other views, and towards the range of human knowledge that has become too great for any individual to grasp. The traditional statements and definitions of faith also lack a close relationship with life itself. Finally, there is the important question of the salvific existential meaning of a historical event: in this case, the event of Jesus.

If we are to understand Rahner's solution to this problem, we cannot escape a preliminary consideration of the apparatus that he uses, his battery of ideas or his theological method. I have, after all, not yet attempted to explain what he means by such terms as 'transcendentality', the 'transcendental and anthropological method', and so on. We have to understand Rahner's apparatus if we are to understand his theology.

The Apparatus of Rahner's Thought

Before I begin to analyze Rahner's method, it is worth recalling that he has always regarded man primarily as a unity. It is possible to differentiate and to make distinctions, to look at man's existence from various points of view and to stress certain aspects of his being or certain activities or functions; but man, according to Rahner, always continues to be one.

It is precisely this indivisible unity of the human person that makes it difficult to describe Rahner's methodology. Obviously, only one aspect of man can be satisfactorily discussed at a time. This does not mean, however, that we should forget or deny the existence of another aspect. However difficult it may be in practice, the other aspect or aspects must always be taken into account. Man is, for example, always both matter and spirit, body and soul, subject and object, an individual and a member of society, free and unfree, and so on. If I try, in this analysis of Rahner's method, to gain at least a preliminary access to his thought, by making a distinction between what is *a priori* and what is *a posteriori* in man, it must be constantly borne in mind that, despite all justified distinctions, the human person or subject is constituted and expressed by the unity and close bond that exists between *a priori* and *a posteriori* elements.

Rahner recognizes *a priori* structures in man and agrees that the term *a priori* (and especially the philosophical term) points to something in man or connected with him that is already present and previously given, something, in other words, that has not simply been acquired on the basis of experience. Nevertheless, he assumes almost unquestioningly that man is in the first place always concerned with the world in which he lives and which forms the basis of his experience. Rahner completely rejects the idea that man comes into the world with innate concepts.[7] In his view, man always acts within the world of his own experience and, what is even more important in this context, has no knowledge that is not mediated to him somehow by way of his senses. His knowledge is therefore always connected with the world of his experience.

All knowledge and all experience that man gains in his world, then, are *a posteriori* knowledge or experience. Rahner calls the whole actual world of man's experience, the

Definition of Categorial

world in which man thinks, lives, and acts, the world of men and things and our own knowledge, experiences, and innermost thoughts—everything, in other words, that man gains in and from his world—'categorial'. (He uses this term in contrast to the term 'transcendental', which I shall discuss in more detail in the following section.)

The term 'categorial', then, points to man's actual, empirical, spatio-temporal reality, in other words, to the world as we know it. Man's history also forms part of this categorial reality, with the result that the expression 'categorial' means not only what is already present in the world of man's own experience, but what he himself has done and is, as a historical act, the objectivization of what he desires in freedom.

One further aspect of Rahner's thought remains to be discussed briefly in this section. Expressions of man's person such as love, faithfulness, and thanksgiving are in the first place expressions of an inner attitude. But they are not simply this. Anyone who loves or is faithful or thankful must also show his love, faithfulness, or thankfulness. He cannot allow them to remain concealed in an innermost and unconscious corner of his heart. This showing of love, faithfulness and other inner attitudes is an 'objectivization'. In such an objectivization, an attitude becomes visible, tangible, and perceptible by the senses.

Rahner even applies the term 'categorial' to concepts. Concepts are not, in his opinion, simply derived in one way or another from human experience and therefore *a posteriori*. They are also an explicit grasping of what man may already know in some sense without being able to conceptualize and therefore to express it.

We may conclude this section by giving a few examples of expressions in which Rahner uses the word 'categorial'. These expressions should be readily understood in the light of what we have said above: 'categorial object', the 'world of categories', 'categorial exposition or interpretation' (which means the same, in Rahner's terminology, as 'categorial objectivization'), 'categorial appearance' and 'categorial conceptuality'.

The Anthropological Approach

Now that I have examined the meanings of the terms in Rahner's apparatus, I can go on to discuss this theological method. I have called this his anthropological approach to theology. The categorial world in which man lives is, after all, always changing. It is a world that is determined by history and subject to historical conditions. Rahner is convinced that a theologian's work must be firmly oriented towards contemporary man. It must address him within the framework of his own experience and mediate faith to him within that framework. For these reasons, Rahner has always used man as the point of departure for all his theological arguments. He has never made use of a 'theoretical' man. On the contrary, his starting-point has inevitably been questions about man as he actually is and the way in which he experiences his existence.

What is man's experience of himself and his world? How does he experience his life? This is where Rahner constantly begins his theology. These and similar questions are asked repeatedly and often form the basis for his treatment of individual theological problems. What is more, Rahner always considers man's experience as historical experience. Man does not experience any period in history in precisely the same way, and it has become a methodological principle for Rahner always to question what has apparently been accepted unquestioningly in the Church's teaching. He does this by testing that traditional teaching about faith against man's experience of himself in the modern world.

These questions are penetrating and persistent. How does modern man react, for example, to this or that statement about faith or to this or that dogmatic pronouncement? What are the causes of resistance when he hears such statements? In what ways are these statements difficult or impossible to believe, alien to or in some way not in accordance with his experience of life today? How does contemporary man understand himself at all? How does he react to experience?

All these and other questions are asked by Rahner, and they form, either explicitly or implictly, the point of departure for his theology. It is therefore quite correct to speak in his case of an anthropological approach—an approach based firmly on man. (Anthropology is, after all, the philosophical study of man.) Rahner's first step towards overcoming the process of incrustation and ossification of Christian teaching has therefore been a hard and unrelenting confrontation between concrete dogmatic pronouncements and the experience of contemporary man. The second step has often enough been an observation that these pronouncements cannot be made to agree with man's experience today, and even that they are apparently irreconcilably opposed to each other.

In this way, then, Rahner breaks radically with the traditional theology of the Church, which did not begin from below, that is, with man himself, but has always insisted that dogmatic statements had to be taught to man in the form in which they had been received in the Church. Rahner's approach is quite different. Man is at the beginning for him, not the Church's statement of faith.[8] His method is to distance the enquiry from dogmatic statement and to direct it to modern man's actual experience. As we have seen, he regards man as a whole and recognizes that, in contemporary society, he has particular experiences, a distinctive way of thinking, a great deal of knowledge, certain reservations, often a one-sided lack of balance, and a strong tinge of scepticism. He is also in a situation of crisis with regard to faith. Rahner therefore concludes that precisely this twentieth-century man's understanding of himself must be seriously questioned. He rejects the argument that this approach may damage faith itself. It is quite safe to begin a justification of faith with man himself, he has argued. No one need fear that his anthropological approach will of necessity lead to a subjective or historically conditioned reduction of Christian faith. This is what he himself has said of his own method and perhaps we should take him at his word.

What has been called the art of hermeneutics and the analysis of human existence also form part of Rahner's anthropological approach to theology. He is quite capable of distinguishing between man's common and universal experience and the type of human experience that is merely historically conditioned and may therefore be transitory. For this reason he has attempted to separate what constitutes man as such from what is characteristic of man in the twentieth century as conditioned by his contemporary situation.

Rahner has succeeded brilliantly in delineating this conditioning of modern man by the contemporary situation, both in its linguistic formulation and in his presentation of the characteristic aspects of the age in which we are living. In a consideration of the historical nature of theology, for example, he has drawn attention to three striking aspects of the modern era: its rational and scientific world-view, with its decisive influence on the thinking of contemporary man; modern man's historical consciousness, and the deeply rooted attitude that accompanies this, resulting in the conviction that there is nothing new in the world; and finally twentieth-century man's overpowering need to plan and create both himself and the world around him.

To this description of man, as determined by the contemporary historical situation, and his attitude towards society and the environment in which he finds himself, Rahner has added, as it were in brackets, this pertinent comment. It is that we have to disregard the fundamental change that has taken place in man's world-view from the cosmocentric attitude of the ancient world and the Middle Ages to the anthropocentricity of the modern era. In other words, we must leave out of account the explicitly transcendental problem of the modern world.

The most pertinent analyses of the existence of twentieth-century man that Rahner provides can be found in his more spiritual writings, to which, unfortunately, I cannot refer here, even briefly. One is bound to ask in this context whether he learnt the art of analyzing man's existence from Martin Heidegger, under whom he studied philosophy. Much of his work is reminiscent of Heidegger and many of the terms that he uses are Heideggerian. He frequently speaks, for example, of 'existence' and 'existential'. In the end, however, it is only a matter of historical interest whether Rahner's masterly skill in describing and analyzing our existence is the result of his own genius, a deep study of Heidegger's philosophy, or a mixture of both.

More important is the fact that Rahner is convinced that this anthropological approach to theology is the direct result and the logical consequence of a definite philosophical and theological method. It does not depend on a philosophical system. Rahner rejects an indissoluble link between theology and a particular philosophical system in the belief that such a close connection must inevitably lead to another incrustation of theological ideas. Let us, in the following section, turn our minds to his transcendental and anthropological method in theology. His thinking is even more clearly determined by this method than by his anthropological approach and he believes, moreover, that it can always be found in theology, though not always so explicitly as in his own work. What, then, is involved in Rahner's transcendental and anthropological method in theology?

The Transcendental and Anthropological Method

Rahner is familiar with the situation in which man finds himself today. He does not try to escape from its reality or seek refuge in statements about faith that simply have to be taught, learnt, and accepted. His solution to this problem is the anthropological approach. Nevertheless, the main emphasis in Rahner's theology is on man's fundamental and constant experiences which, as we have already seen, are always the same, however much they may be determined by the historical situation. Contemporary man is never simply and solely contemporary man, Rahner has often pointed out, and is never a mere product of historical, sociological, psychological, biological, or any other conditioning. He has frequently declared that theology will in the future be even more explicitly a transcendental theology. What, then, is this transcendental theology?

In any attempt to answer this question, we must first of all bear in mind that one of Rahner's most important presuppositions is that we are very much concerned in this life with man and with the concrete things in the world of our experience, in other words, with the categorial reality. What, then, does he mean when he postulates an *a priori* datum in man and speaks not only of a categorial reality, but of a transcendental reality or experience?

When he speaks of an *a priori* datum, Rahner means something that is not acquired by man simply as a result of his association with the world of experience. It is something that precedes that association, and not simply in the temporal sense. Without the *a posteriori* experiences that man has, nothing can really be known about his *a priori* constitution.

(I have already pointed to the interrelationship of the two.) The *a priori* aspect of our knowledge and activity is, however, not constituted by the *a posteriori* reality and categorial experiences and objectivizations. On the contrary, it has to be said that, on closer inspection, it can be seen from the categorial reality itself (which is, as I have already pointed out, the actual world of everyday human experience), that we are not simply and solely concerned here with this categorial reality, but that our human knowledge and activity, our experiences and our fate as human beings would not be possible without the presupposition of an *a priori* element in man: that is, an innate element preceding all that is acquired in the world of experience.

This may strike anyone who is not particularly skilled in philosophy as remarkable and I am therefore bound to explain what it means. It should be remembered that Jürgen Habermas began his book *Knowledge and Interest* with the statement that a reconstruction of contemporary philosophical debate in the form of a case in the law court would result in an appeal being made to the idea, which could be applied in any need to decide about a single question, namely: how reliably knowledge may be possible. It would not be wrong to complete Habermas' statement by qualifying: '. . . if knowledge is possible at all'.

It should be borne in mind that, in the explanation of Rahner's theological method in the paragraphs that follow, the aim of this transcendental and anthropological method can be clarified by one of those images that can be found without too much difficulty in Rahner's repertoire. In one article, for example, on man's experience of God, he has spoken of being able to be even more concrete with regard to the simple concentration of ultimate experience present everywhere in man's everyday experience, and in which man lives on the beach of the infinite sea of mystery, busy with the grains of sand he finds there.

Let us therefore consider the aim of this transcendental method. A knowledge of this aim may make it easier for us to understand the method itself and its terminology. It is possible to claim that the aim of this method is to show that man's task in life is not primarily to be busy with the grains of sand that he finds on the beach, but to live on the beach of the infinite sea of mystery. In other words, the aim is to demonstrate that knowledge, experience, and activity would simply not be possible for man if all that he had in his hands were the grains of sand that he found in his everyday life on the beach. There is an *a priori* element in man that makes it possible for him to experience his existence in the way in which he in fact does experience it. It is the aim of Rahner's theological method to elaborate and clarify the meaning of this *a priori* element and to show that it exists. Part of this aim is also to point out precisely what it is in man and what its origin is.

This can be made clear on the basis of the relationship outlined above between history and the existential meaning of this contingent or coincidental history. Rahner knows that there are thousands of questions in human life which do not urgently require an answer or an explanation. He makes a clear distinction between positive factual knowledge and what is of existential significance for man. One of Rahner's own examples may help to make this clear. It makes little difference to man whether he knows that there are opossums in Australia or whether he does not know this fact. This and similar knowledge usually comes within the category of what man can ask or not, and what he can know or not, without that asking and knowing influencing his actual attitude towards life or his management of his own existence. Not all questions are, however, equally unimportant. What is truth? Can it be known? What is the situation with regard to human freedom and responsibility? Does God exist? What is the significance of guilt, love, faithfulness, hope, and so on? These are questions which are qualitatively different and from which man—and Rahner himself—cannot escape so easily.

Of course, not everything can be called into question in Rahner's transcendental method; this includes positive factual knowledge of the kind that can only be gained by scientific investigation or experience of life. We should, however, bear in mind that there are, as we have already seen, certain things in life which we cannot overlook or escape. History is important in this context because it may provide the answer to those questions which we do not, as it were, invent—and which are for this reason given *a priori* with man's existence—and which we cannot, moreover, escape. If history is able to provide us with a definitive and reliable answer to our questions about truth, love, hope, and so on, then we must conclude that history is not of secondary importance, but of great importance and, in certain circumstances, of decisive importance for man's life. This, of course, presupposes that man can never be exclusively preoccupied with the grains of sand on the beach of everyday life, that is, exclusively involved in categorial and *a posteriori* activities, but that he also has an *a priori* constitution, something that Rahner calls 'transcendental'. I shall examine this concept more closely a little further on, but before I do so, I must consider one final aspect of his aim in using the transcendental method.

The transcendental method—the word 'method' would itself suggest this—does not in the first place provide a content or make any statements. It is rather a certain way of asking. Man's *a priori* constitution can be regarded as the supra-historical aspect of man (although not as something that is above or beyond history). In the same way, the aim of the transcendental method is a purposeful questioning of man's supra-historical dimension. To express this in a more concrete way, it is a questioning of what may be called the conditioning of the possibility of human knowledge and human activity.

This phrase, 'the conditioning of the possibility', which derives from Kant, is undoubtedly a key-word in any attempt to explain the meaning of Rahner's transcendental method. Because the word 'transcendental' has so many levels of meaning, it is in itself difficult to understand, but it occurs so frequently in Rahner's theological writings and is of such obvious importance that an attempt has to be made to define it.

The word is obviously derived from the Latin *transcendere*, to transcend, and points in Rahner's theology to man's supra-historical and dynamic orientation, already present *a priori* in his constitution—towards a reality that transcends the empirically historical world. Rahner uses it in such combinations as 'transcendental method', 'transcendental and anthropological questioning', 'transcendental experience', 'transcendental reflection', 'transcendental reduction' and 'transcendental subject'. He also refers frequently to man's 'transcendentality'. 'Transcendence' in his vocabulary usually points to the objective reality of God. At first sight, this may seem confusing, but the confusion disappears to some extent if the origin of the term in the history of philosophy is borne in mind.

Kant, Maréchal and Rahner

Rahner has frequently drawn attention to the 'anthropological change', or the 'change to the subject' as a critical point in the history of man's ideas that cannot and should not be reversed. This idea of turning towards the subject was first introduced by Descartes and later developed by Kant. It is also marked by a turning away from a naive realism in which human knowledge is presented as an image, that is, as though man's brain were an image in miniature of what man himself knows.

The Kantian theory developed in the *Critique of Pure Reason* is, of course, too complex to be outlined in full here, but I can at least point out that it can be understood as an explicit question about the conditions of the possibility—or the presuppositions—that have to be present in the knowing subject for man to be able to know and judge at all, especially in cases where a datum of knowledge or judgment contains more than can be mediated simply by sense-perception. (Space prevents me from discussing here whether this exists or not.) In other words, Kant believed that human knowledge was, as it were, composed of two factors: the passive acceptance (or perception) of an object and the active participation of the knowing subject, which may or may not be explicitly desired or conscious on the part of that subject. Whenever man knows something, he never has, in that knowledge, the pure reality alone—the famous Kantian thing in itself. What happens is that a subjective aspect also flows into the knowledge and the judgment itself. This subjective aspect is not the result of knowledge, experience or perception; it is something that is always present in man. It is, in other words, an *a priori* element of human knowledge. To put it very crudely, whatever object man observes, he automatically makes a connection between it and certain 'categories' or previously existing structures of his capacity to know. It is only in this way that it is possible for him to know and judge. These judgments are what Kant called 'synthetic judgments *a priori*'. It is, moreover, precisely in this context that Kant used the term 'transcendental': 'I call all knowledge that is concerned not with objects, but with our way of knowing objects, insofar as these are possible, *a priori*, transcendental'.[9] Since Kant first used it at the end of the eighteenth century, the term 'transcendental' has become a key-word in philosophy.

Kant was anxious to demonstrate that this *a priori* human knowledge applied in the same way to all men, since this was the only possible explanation of the fact that mathematics and physics, for example, were acknowledged by all men to be empirically correct. If each individual had an *a priori* subjective structure of knowledge that was different from that of other individuals, this fact would remain inexplicable. In the sense in which Kant used the word, then, 'transcendental' also has a horizontal meaning—it is necessarily and inevitably present *a priori* in all men. We must now return to Rahner's transcendental method and consider how Kant's term is employed by Rahner.

The term 'transcendental' is still used by most philosophers in the Kantian sense, and misunderstandings inevitably arise when Rahner's use of the word is mistakenly thought to be purely Kantian. It is important to remember that Rahner's transcendental subject is not simply identical with Kant's transcendental subject. This difference in usage can be explained by the fact that Rahner has followed the unfortunately too little known Belgian Jesuit philosopher and theologian Joseph Maréchal to such an extent that he can quite legitimately be regarded as his disciple. In Maréchal's teaching, and consequently in Rahner's too, the term 'transcendental' has not only a horizontal direction— the only direction permitted in Kant's thought—but a vertical direction. In other words, Maréchal and Rahner acknowledge the possibility of a (metaphysical) knowledge of God.

Such, then, is the principal difference between Rahner's and Kant's use of 'transcendental'. In the more positive sense, Rahner made use of a number of aspects that were sketched out by Kant and incorporated them into his transcendental method. For example, Rahner's thought is firmly directed towards the subject and the 'conditions of the possibility' of human knowledge, freedom, and other experiences. What conditions, in other words, must be present for man to be able to do this or that particular thing, act in this or that way or experience himself and his life in this or that manner?

Again and again Rahner's anthropological approach breaks through and discloses new depths because of Rahner's own experience. He is concerned less with the historical conditions governing man as a transcendental subject, since these are always changing, than with the inevitable structures without which man's spiritual and intellectual activities cannot be understood. Rahner has also taken over from Kant the question of the conditions of the possibility of knowledge. However difficult the following paragraph based on Rahner's theology may be, it has importance, because it throws light on his understanding of this problem.

Whatever the sphere of objective knowledge may be, Rahner has pointed out, a transcendental question always arises in the case of the conditions of the possibility of knowing a certain object in the knowing subject. Generally speaking, Rahner maintains, it is not necessary or even possible to discuss whether this question is fundamentally justified. Both what is known and the knowing subject are involved in knowledge, which is in turn dependent not only on the qualities of the objects, but on the essential structure of the knowing subject. The mutual relationship between the knowing subject and the known object as something that is known and capable of being known is the object of a transcendental question. In the mutual relationship between *a priori*, transcendental subjectivity and the object of knowledge (and freedom), Rahner insists, knowledge of the *a priori* conditions of the possibility of knowledge in the subject are of necessity also an aspect of our knowledge of the object itself, both with regard to the question of the metaphysically necessary being of the object that is known and with regard to the question of the concrete historical character of the object that is not necessary. A transcendental question is therefore not a question in addition to the one about the original, *a posteriori* and empirical object, but an expression of the full being of our knowledge of the original object itself. Knowledge of the knowing subject, Rahner concludes, is always at the same time a knowledge of the metaphysical—and therefore in an objective sense transcendental—structures of the object itself.

Rahner points here to the fact there is also an objective use of the word 'transcendental'. In so doing, he makes a distinction between his own thought and that of Kant and gives a different meaning to the word, one that Kant explicitly rejected, namely the vertical meaning, the sense of pointing upwards. Rahner, then, clearly also recognizes that 'transcendental' never refers exclusively to the question of the subjective conditions of the possibility of knowing and acting. In his thought, it is never simply a question about the transcendental subject, as it was for Kant. The vertical meaning is always also present—the idea of transcendence above all categorial, empirical experience.

This is, of course, because Rahner believes that it is possible to have metaphysical knowledge of God. For him, God is the presupposition, the 'condition of the possibility' which Kant ultimately simply left unexplained. We shall be considering our knowledge of God in a later chapter; for the present, however, we must try to understand the meaning which Rahner gives to the term 'transcendental' in his theological method. In his teaching, man's transcendentality always also points to man's openness to what he calls 'mystery'. The transcendentality of man's spirituality is the origin and the aim of man's experience. It is what makes it possible for man to be. It is also what exists objectively and independently of man. Man participates in it and is directed towards it, but never in fact has it. Neither man's origin nor his destiny can, in Rahner's opinion, simply be the void, nothingness or non-being; nor can they be no more than a projection of the human spirit that is not in accordance with any objective reality. Transcendence is reality and man is only a transcendental subject because this transcendence exists. In a word, this transcendence is another and more original name for God.

As I said above, our knowledge and experience of God will be discussed in a later chapter, but here I have to go on to consider, in the present context of my examination of Rahner's transcendental method, two further points. The first is concerned with the content of his method. I could answer the question 'What is the content of Rahner's theological method?' crudely, but fairly accurately, by saying that it has no content. This is because, as Rahner has always stressed, man is never able to grasp his *a priori* and transcendental constitution adequately and can never reflect upon it completely. The content of a transcendental reflection is always of secondary importance and is always less than the original datum or the original experience.

What does Rahner mean in this context by 'experience'? When he uses it, for example, in the phrase 'transcendental experience', he is not concerned with man's everyday experience of something new. On the contrary, he is concerned with what man experiences always and transcendentally in himself. Man's transcendental experiences play a most important, if not a central part in Rahner's theology, since his transcendental method is ultimately an elaboration of these transcendental experiences, which are as such not new to man, but are *a priori;* in other words, they have always existed for him. In this context, then, we may say that a step has to be taken in the elaboration of these transcendental experiences from a non-conceptual, non-explicit,

non-systematized, and non-reflective form of knowledge—
as the condition of the possibility of man's conscious
knowing and acting—to a conceptual, explicit, systematic,
and reflective form of knowledge.

This is bound to strike the reader who is still unfamiliar
with the works of Rahner as complicated. The whole
problem will be discussed at greater depth later, but in the
meantime it is worth pointing out that he never ceases to
insist that such transcendental experiences exist and to give
examples and analogies to illustrate their existence.

Man already experiences joy, fear, faithfulness, love, and
so on, as well as logical thought and responsible decisions,
long before reflecting about these experiences and trying to
express what took place within them. In any case, Rahner
has pointed out, reflection or pronouncements about such
experiences may well be false or insufficient. It is possible,
for example, for real, personal love to be experienced on a
particular occasion and yet for quite a false statement to be
made when one is asked what in fact happened on that
occasion. It is equally possible to say something quite
pertinent and intelligent, as a result of indoctrination, even
if one has had no experience at all of the matter under
discussion.

We may therefore conclude that the transcendental
method does not lead directly to a statement about content.
The *a priori* structure of my knowledge and activity is a
non-explicit datum that is experienced and of which I am
conscious at the same time. It would therefore be wrong to
think that anything concrete and tangible that can be
expressed precisely exists in connection with man's transcendentality. It is only possible to understand it when we
begin to ask questions about the conditions of the possibility
of our experiences. Bearing Rahner's examples in mind, this
means that I can think logically without being explicitly
conscious of the fact that I am thinking logically. I can love

without having reflected explicitly about what love is. I can also look for truth or be worried or bored without being explicitly conscious of what I am doing, or without being able to say precisely what I am doing.

Rahner has called man's transcendental consciousness, which is also present in categorial experience and which has also been gained in that experience, the sphere of understanding; by this he means the sphere within which the things of our concrete life take place unconsciously and unnoticed. These events are enacted, as it were, on a stage, but those who are taking part in the play are no longer explicitly conscious of everything that they see and hear around them as simply taking place on the stage. It may therefore happen that a man 'acts' on the stage of his life for a whole lifetime without ever being explicitly conscious of the fact that there could be no 'play of life' without a stage.

Another comparison—one that has been used for a long time in the history of faith—is light. We cannot see without light, yet, in ordinary everyday life, we do not think about the fact that we can only see the objects that surround us because of the existence of light. The stage and light—these and other examples have been used by Rahner to illustrate that there are things in our life that are a presupposition for that life, but at the same time that we are normally not explicitly conscious that these things exist and that we need them. We only become conscious of them when we reflect and enquire about the conditions of the possibility of knowledge and experience. What is more, our understanding of these experiences can never be fully reflected or unambiguously expressed. We all know in some way or another what happiness is or means, but whenever we try to express that happiness, for example, in words, we recognize that our words are insufficient and do not quite cover the experience itself. Rahner has therefore commented, in this context, that there can be reflection about experience at the transcendental level of objective knowledge; and that that experience can be presented systematically and conceptually and even made an explicit object of knowledge; but that this can only take place within the transcendental sphere, and that sphere can never be systematic.

Man is always transcendental, Rahner has frequently stressed, because he could not otherwise be what he is. At the same time, however, the transcendental sphere of his conscious knowledge and activity is never fully known and can never be adequately understood, even when we reflect deeply about the condition of the possibility of knowledge and action. Although I shall discuss this question more fully later on, for the present we may assume that man's transcendental experience—his non-explicit consciousness of his transcendentality—is, according to Rahner, his experience of God, and this can be used as a basis for elucidating the meaning of what has been said so far.

If, then, man has experience of God, but at the same time it is not possible to express the reality of God adequately in words and concepts—because these have a limiting factor— then it is clear that man's transcendentality, as a participation in God's transcendence, also cannot be adequately expressed in words and concepts. In Rahner's view, what makes it possible for man to be a man is his participation in and reference to a transcendental reality. He regards it as of secondary importance to ask whether the infinite space revealed in this movement as being without boundaries or end is the void that points to infinite fulness because nothingness is not able to extend itself as a space of the possibility of this experience, or to say that this aim is itself revealed as infinite fulness.

It is therefore also a question of secondary importance, Rahner has pointed out, to make a clear distinction between experience of God and experience of being referred to God. It is necessary to make a distinction between objective and subjective aspects of experience, in order to distinguish man from God, but it is, in Rahner's view, essential to recognize that these two aspects are, in a unique and original way, inseparable from each other. It is also important to remember that this experience of God cannot be fully explained or proved. Rahner's transcendental method is fundamentally a form of questioning and elaborating what has to be present in order that man should be what he is and how he is, and so that he is able to experience himself in the way that he does. His transcendental method can only show that our concrete experience, with which we are primarily concerned in life and with which, it would seem at first sight, we are exclusively concerned, is not able to understand or explain man's being as a total reality. It also shows that what is already given is, in fact, always given—it is the condition of the possibility, in Rahner's words—but that it is not normally explicitly known. It can be known only in reflection, but even then it can never be completely understood or expressed in words and concepts.

A great deal of what I have said so far about Rahner's transcendental method and the originality of his theological thought will be made clear in the chapters that follow, when I shall try to show how his method is used. It will be to the reader's advantage therefore to refer back to this first chapter from time to time as he reads on. In the meantime, however, I must draw his attention to another important aspect of Rahner's method.

As I have already indicated, Rahner regards transcendental experience and experience of God as materially the same. In this context, he has also declared that experience of God is a question of transcendental necessity. Although it is usually not systematic, it is, he is convinced, present everywhere and at all times, wherever man is spiritually free and has knowledge. It is also present even if he systematically, verbally and objectively denies this transcendentally necessary relationship with God. If this transcendental necessity is in fact denied, God is understood as a random object, and man's experience of him can be permitted or avoided with equal justification. A claim to God's objective and overriding importance would be too late, Rahner thinks, to justify the necessity of our experience of God.

In addition to this, Rahner tries, with his transcendental method, to prove that man's transcendental experience is inevitable. This aim is so important a part of the method that a transcendental question is seen to be transcendental if we are unable to avoid it, even though we may behave as if we can in fact avoid it. As I have already observed, not everything can be called into question by the transcendental method. But Rahner is convinced that there are certain questions—or, as he calls them, 'experiences'—which no one can in the long run avoid. Such questions cannot be permanently thrust into the background. Even if they are totally suppressed, or we deny their significance, or say that some kind of answer has already been provided, these questions go on being asked in the depths of our existence.

Rahner's argument in this context is that there are experiences that are gained as such if they are wrongly interpreted, denied, or suppressed in reflection. We may, for example, claim that there is no logic and no truth that is fundamentally different from error, and that what we call logic or truth is really only the product of certain mechanical functions of the brain or certain social compulsions, which might easily have been different. If we make this claim, we are in fact making a statement the opposite of which we are asserting to be wrong, but we are experiencing again, whether we admit it or not, the claim made by truth and absolute logic which we are denying in our reflective statement.

This insight into the inevitability of certain experiences enables us to be more precise about the transcendental method used by Rahner. It is possible to know in this and similar ways, within more and more clearly defined limits, the extent of what can and should be called into question by this method. Various elements are revealed that were initially concealed: what motivates man, for example, and the factors to which he is inevitably bound to react, even when he suppresses or tries to suppress questions and answers.

The title of this chapter is 'from necessity to method' and in it I have tried to outline both the necessity for a new way of thinking about faith in view of the contemporary crisis, and Rahner's response to this challenge by evolving his own theological method. Rahner's own name for this method— as we have seen, he describes it as a 'transcendental and anthropological method of theology'—is an apt and concise definition. The anthropological approach in his theology is unmistakable. Man in his contemporary situation and with his contemporary experiences is the point of departure. His self-understanding has to be questioned so that statements about faith may once again be significant and have a bearing on his life today.

Modern man is, however, never simply and solely modern man. There is a reality in man that belongs to humanity as such. This is the presupposition or 'condition of the possibility' for everything that man does, knows, experiences, suffers and hopes. This reality is what Rahner calls 'transcendental' and it can be questioned with the help of his transcendental method. Rahner did not invent this method himself,[10] but he was the first to introduce it into theology. With his stubborn and persistent questioning and his refusal to be satisfied with superficial answers, he has added dimensions to theology that were unthinkable a few decades ago. He has, in so doing, performed a very valuable service to our understanding of faith, a service that forms part of his aim as an 'amateur' theologian.

The most important word that we have had to discuss in
this first chapter is 'transcendental'. We can summarize its
meaning as an *a priori* structure of human knowledge and
activity that is not acquired in the first place from experience
(although it is knowable in experience and, through reflection, by way of experience). This *a priori* structure is the
condition of the possibility of this human knowledge and
activity (and therefore of humanity as such).

This 'transcendental' element is inevitably and necessarily
present in every man, but it is impossible to understand and
reflect about it adequately. It cannot, in other words, be
reduced to words and concepts that will sufficiently reflect its
depth and full content. This is because, in Rahner's terminology at least, the term 'transcendental' has not only a
horizontal, but a vertical meaning. It points to a reality that
is simply inexpressible because it does not belong to this
world and transcends all categorial elements. As a special
mode of questioning, then, the transcendental method tries
to show that there must be such an *a priori* structure in man
and that this is at the same time a way of participating in the
transcendental reality of God.

·2·

But We Know Nothing
about Man...

These words are taken from the title of a book by the
biologist and philosopher, L. von Bertalanffy, and I
have quoted them because Rahner would undoubtedly
agree with them. We know a great deal more about man now
than we did in the past, of course, but the question still
remains: Who—or what—is man?

The transcendental method, as applied by Rahner to
theology, has to prove its value in practice. As we have
already seen, the approach in this method is anthropological. Indeed, Rahner is convinced that dogmatic theology
must be 'theological anthropology' and that a theological
change of this kind is both necessary and fruitful. This
theological anthropology is bound to make us question man,
because, as Rahner himself has said, God's Word became
man and we inevitably ask what it means: became *man*. We
do not ask what it means when we say that this Word
'became' something. We look above all at *what* the Word
became. He became, Rahner has said, man. And here
Rahner asks: Do we understand this? We can say, for
example, that the most understandable part of this statement is man. Man is, he points out, what we are, what we
experience in our lives every day, what has been tried out
and interpreted a thousand or more times already in the

history of which we form a part. Man is what we know from within—in each individual experience—and from without—from our environment. We know very many different things about man, of course, but does this necessarily mean, Rahner asks, that man is defined? His answer to this question is a clear negative, as we shall see further on.

This chapter has two principal aims. In the first place, an attempt is made to show that man cannot be defined and that he is fundamentally open and oriented. In the second place, and connected with this first aim, we shall try to understand the datum of this openness and orientation, and the reasons for them, by elucidating man's transcendental experiences.

The Question about Man

Rahner's original intention was to teach philosophy, not theology, and he has brought to theology his philosophical knowledge of the transcendental method. No method, however, and certainly no specific philosophical method, is for Rahner an end in itself. Transcendental questioning of man has to prove its value. For Rahner the theologian, this means that transcendental questioning has to prove its worth with regard to man's question about God on the one hand and with regard to the problem of nature and grace on the other. As we shall see later on, these two questions are ultimately identical in Rahner's thinking.

Rahner, who is very conscious of the urgency of man's question about God today, can only approach this question by asking in the first place about man. It is above all here that the fruitfulness and effectiveness of his anthropological approach are demonstrated, since, in a sense, all theological questions begin with the question about God. All other theological questions are fundamentally simply a develop-

ment of this one question. What is more, the question about
God must also begin with the question about man, although
modern man should not think that the reality of God enters
his life for the first time when he hears from outside—by
indoctrination—that there is or may be something like
'God'.

Rahner himself has said that theology often gives the
impression nowadays of providing mythological or at least
unscientific answers to questions which can either only be
answered by scientists or else have a meaning that cannot be
expressed in any known way. Theology, he claims, also
strikes modern man as a complex network of concepts
closed to verification and arbitrarily supported by the
obscure and unreflecting levels of human experience that
have not yet been or cannot be clarified by anthropological
studies and therefore cannot be used.

Rahner believes that the theologian can only overcome
this impression that theology is simply a tissue of concepts,
especially in its treatment of the question about God, by
beginning with man and his experiences. If this approach is
followed, God ceases to be merely the name given to a reality
that enters man's life subsequently, giving rise to a question
about the meaning of that reality in his life. The anthropological approach points to God above all—whatever man
may be able to learn about God from revelation—as having
his ground in human experience. Man has therefore to
learn from his own experience who or what God is. Any
attempt to justify the existence of God without this human
experience would be valueless.

Man's Openness

Rahner regards man as essentially open and therefore as
impossible to define. What does he mean by this openness?
Man seems to be open to everything. Nothing completely

ever open to more Knowledge

↓

deeper + fuller experience

satisfies or fulfils him. There are always spheres of knowledge that remain hidden from him. There are always questions to which there is no immediate answer. Man has experiences, but knows that he continues to be open to an even greater fulness of experience and a greater and different fulfilment. There is no love that does not make him hope for a greater and more lasting love. There is no human faithfulness that does not impel him to seek complete security. In his book *Christian at the Crossroads,* Rahner has written: 'What is man? In my answer to this question, I will not beat about the bush. I believe that man is the question to which there is no answer. Why? It is true that every man has a great number of experiences in the course of his life and in this way comes to know a little about himself. It is also true that the results of the different anthropological sciences teach us more and more about man and that our knowledge will continue to increase as these sciences expand. It is also true to say that there is a branch of anthropology that is metaphysical and theological and I do not think that all the findings made in that sphere are meaningless or uncertain!'

None of this, Rahner has insisted again and again, can ever provide us with a formula about man. Not even he, with his insights into metaphysical anthropology, is able to define man. A little further on in the same book, he says: 'If those specializing in metaphysical anthropology understand man correctly, they must see him as a being of unlimited transcendentality, as the spiritual subject that transcends, in his questioning, every individual—and finite—object (and is therefore a spirit), and as a being that can nowhere come to a definitive halt. This infinite extent of possible knowledge, insights and experiences, however, can never be fulfilled and completed on its own. The space in which life, experience, knowledge, happiness, and sorrow are stored is infinite and is therefore always half empty—and this is based on the most optimistic calculation'.

This human openness, which can be empirically verified, is for Rahner fundamental to man's essential being which, by virtue of this openness, can never be fully defined or expressed. To quote again from the same book: 'Because we always go beyond every finite object, but at the same time always seize hold only of such finite objects, we are never finished in finite time and every end is merely a beginning. This is the reason for our terrible boredom. We go on storing more and more new experiences in our consciousness and it disappears in its infinite space, which always, as it were, remains empty. We go on running, but remain on the same spot'.

It is, then, never possible to say definitively who man is. This fundamental openness of man's being towards what is constantly new—this new experience and new fulfilment that never come to an end—has to be included in any definition of man. This is precisely what Rahner does, because this fundamental openness is based on an orientation towards what is nameless and inexpressible. It remains to be seen whether this nameless and inexpressible mystery of man's orientation is really God, or whether this experience can be differently interpreted.

In the meantime, one thing is quite clear—Rahner would not agree with Wittgenstein or the modern linguistic analysts[11] that the limits of man's language are the limits of his world (*Tractatus logico-philosophicus*, 5. 6) or with Wittgenstein's statement: 'What we cannot talk about we must consign to silence' (*ibid.*, introduction).

There can also be little doubt that Rahner is, in many respects, a rationalist. He has several times called himself such. He is convinced that a Christian's faith must be questioned by his reason and justified in rational honesty.

Nothing is more alien to his spirit than a theological
positivism which is unable to justify faith or a fideism which
attempts to justify faith by feelings that cannot be rationally
justified. He is, all the same, passionately committed to
talking about what cannot be talked about,[12] and he does this
on the basis of a conviction he fully shares with Gadamer:
'Every one of us must accept the verifiability of all knowledge within the limits of what is possible as an ideal. But at
the same time we must also recognize that this ideal is
seldom achieved and that those experts who try to achieve
this idea in the most precise form usually fail to tell us the
most important things'.[13]

We may conclude this section with a number of comments
made by Rahner himself on man's openness. He believes,
for instance, that we have already spoken about the inexpressible mystery when we are in fact prevented from
speaking. If rationalists and positivists do not speak about it,
will saints, poets and others who reveal the whole of man's
existence let themselves be silenced? Will the word God,
which, after all, exists and is used in the struggle against God
conducted by atheists, not continue to evoke the question as
to what is meant by it? Even if the word 'God' were
forgotten, Rahner declares, the nameless and inexpressible
mystery of our existence would still continue to surround us,
silently leading us to ultimate freedom and grace and be
present above all in the decisive moments of our lives, and
we should rediscover the old name for it.

Modern man, Rahner has pointed out, is still a rationalist
who experiences the world not as numinous, but as material
to be explored by science and technology. He is, however,
not simply and solely a rationalist. He is less of a rationalist
than his spiritual ancestors in the eighteenth and nineteenth
centuries. He is aware of and venerates the nameless and
inexpressible mystery. This, at least, is Rahner's observation

and it would seem to be confirmed by the waves of religiosity inside and outside the churches in recent years.

Theology as a Science?

It is precisely because there are things we cannot talk about but cannot consign to silence that Rahner believes that the distinctive characteristic of theology as a science is to keep the question about man open. It is, in his opinion, precisely this that distinguishes theology from the other sciences. He contrasts theology with the common contemporary attitude, according to which man's openness and indefinable quality are merely that part of him that has not yet been fully understood. He says that, confronted with this attitude, theology can only go over to a determined counter-attack, armed with transcendental reason. In this attack, it can assert that mystery is not just another word for what has not yet been fully understood, but something that can be explicitly accepted.

Theology is a science, Rahner has always insisted, but not a science that is only concerned with sharpening knives. It is a science in which cutting has ultimately to be done. Although he sees scientific research as a necessary part of the theologian's task, Rahner does not think the real aim of theology as a science is to elaborate an increasingly specialized conceptual apparatus, or to deal with themes that are only of interest to specialist theologians and intelligible only to them.

Intellectual Honesty

It is not only the task of defending man's understanding of himself against sciences which try to explain the phenomenon of man in terms of mundane causes that falls to theology. In recent years Rahner has been increasingly concerned with the question of intellectual honesty in theology. The question is fundamentally: How can faith be intellectually honest in view of the pluralism that prevails today, not only in science, but also in philosophy? What is more, how can it be intellectually honest if it is not based on compelling proofs and if it is not able ultimately to appeal only to human freedom?

Rahner leaves no room for doubt regarding the points of departure for any question about an intellectually honest justification of faith. It is no longer possible, as we have seen in the first chapter of this book, for any individual to have a comprehensive understanding of all sciences or to reflect equally deeply about all scientific problems. Because of the pluralism of modern society, we are all amateurs, skating over deep abysses without noticing it. It is not possible to specialize in every field, and yet we ought to. Rahner nonetheless insists that every man has a right and a duty to express his convictions even though he may not have reflected deeply as a specialist about them nor have the ability to express them scientifically. This is because it is simply not possible to reflect adequately about every problem and to objectivize fully everything that is present in one's own consciousness and also because, as Rahner points out, that adequate reflection exists in a finite consciousness and is confronted with a transcendental necessity.

What, then, Rahner asks, is this intellectual honesty? There is a great temptation to think, he has written, that the intellectually honest man is the man who is sceptical and reserved, uncommitted, reluctant to make decisions, and critical, putting everything to the test, avoiding error by ultimately accepting nothing and claiming that what is really the weakness of indecision is the courage of a scepticism without illusion. Certainly, Rahner has pointed out, anyone who honestly believes that he can be no more than a concerned atheist, and who is only conscious of the Medusa's head of the absurdity of human existence, is bound to try to accept this experience calmly. The believer will also recognize that God will bless the atheist for this honest admission. He should not, however, say that this is the only intellectually honest attitude. How could he know that? Rahner asks: How could he ever know that no one has left this Purgatorio or Inferno and that the strength to believe and experience all this does not exist?

Rahner is therefore clearly convinced that it is possible for us to be intellectually honest, even if we have not studied the matter scientifically or reflected about it in great detail and that this intellectual honesty calls for an existential decision that is based less on knowledge than on insight, since knowledge and understanding are not simply identical. Such an existential decision is, of course, always open to doubt. But faith itself is also always open to question and cannot be compelled, however great our knowledge.

Rahner traces this distinction between understanding and knowledge back to faith itself. Faith is, after all, free and is bound to be free if it is to have any significance at all in our lives. According to Rahner, we are nowadays all *rudes,*[14] that is, those who lack a desirable knowledge of faith; but, within the community of believers, this is not a new situation. All that is new is that the theologian himself is also, on the basis of the pluralism of sciences, ignorant and lacking in knowledge of faith. The 'simple' believer can always have an authentic faith, because faith is based not on a knowledge of faith, but on an analogous experience of transcendental experience and categorial experience together, and comes within the sphere of personal expression, which cannot be proved in the interpersonal sphere. Given this basis for faith, then, it is also possible for us to be intellectually honest as contemporary believers, since truth—and this is Rahner's ultimate and fundamental conviction—is always able to prove its validity to man seeking to understand.

It should be clear from what I have said so far that the real
task of theology as a science is, in Rahner's opinion, not to
communicate information or knowledge, but to reveal and
throw light on the experiences that we always have as human
beings. These human, transcendental experiences cannot be
communicated to man as quite new phenomena. It is only
possible to appeal to them in the hope that man, who is
addressed in these appeals, will recognize his own experience and understand it as correctly interpreted. As Rahner
himself has said, reflections of this kind are no more than
indications or addresses, inviting the hearer to attempt to
discover, accept, release and grasp and not to repress this
possibly completely anonymous experience in himself and
to ask himself whether or not he can understand that this
appeal to his experience is a correct interpretation of that
experience.

It is only when man accepts himself as a fundamentally
open being, whose openness cannot be limited in any way,
that religiosity really begins. Rahner claims that man begins
to be *homo religiosus* when he turns towards the question
about questions, the idea of thought and the space of
knowledge and not simply towards the objects of knowledge
and transcendence and towards what is categorially understood in space and time in that transcendence.

Rahner is quite convinced that we can only begin to
understand what is meant by God when we acknowledge
fully that our being is open and cannot be defined. We
should not simply say, he has stressed, that what is experienced in a certain way means God. This presupposes that it
is already clear *a priori* what is meant by God. On the
contrary, Rahner insists, we should rather say: What is
meant by God can be understood in the light of that
experience. If we do not express it in this way, there is
always a danger of thinking of something meaningless when

we use the word God, of rejecting this idea of God and then of thinking that we are atheists.

This insight, namely that God is only a name for human experiences (although not, of course, identical with those experiences) and that man first knows who God is on the basis of those experiences, to such an extent that, if the word 'God' were to be lost, he would find it again, can only be proved true by an analysis of man's transcendental experiences as such.

The aim of these transcendental experiences can be outlined as follows. Superficially and in practice, man is always primarily concerned only with the concrete world of his own experiences, the world, that is, of categorial objects. Looking beneath the surface, however, and in reality, man is also concerned with the previously given, transcendental structure of his own subjectivity. As a condition of the possibility of knowledge and activity, this transcendental structure must be present if man is to know or act at all. This *a priori* structure can, moreover, never be adequately expressed in words and concepts. It transcends the world of categorial reality and is oriented towards something infinite and inexpressible.

This fact was recognized by Kolakowski,[15] who has asked (as has Rahner in connection with human values, logic and the meaning of such concepts as love and freedom) how it is possible to know that relationships that are unworthy of man can and do exist. We cannot know this simply on the basis of concrete, empirical experiences alone. Within history, Kolakowski has said in a comprehensive summary of his ideas, 'which is contained within the limits of events, which may be either enframed in laws or open to explanation on the basis of causes, nothing is due to man, he is called to nothing, no claims are made on him and he is not required to be true, more true or less true as a man. He is what he is at any time and in each case. From the empirical point of view, history is closed in such a way that it has no legal validity, on the basis of which I am able to make claims for mankind or in the name of my fellowmen'.[16]

The concrete, empirical world, then, is always as it is. How can I know what a 'true man' is, at least in the sense that I can know what relationships that are unworthy of man are? Rahner has always been preoccupied with this kind of problem, which is ultimately concerned with man's transcendental experiences or, rather, with the need to make man aware of the fact that he is not exclusively involved in a purely categorial world.

Rahner's Analysis of Man's Transcendental Experiences

If we are to understand Rahner's theology at all, we cannot avoid examining, however briefly, man's transcendental experiences. As we have already seen, these are present in the form of a non-systematic sphere of knowledge and as the condition of the possibility of man's categorial activity. Rahner is conscious of the fact that to insist that such human experiences exist is to encounter opposition in a world which is firmly oriented towards positivism. In *The Spirit in the Church* (pp. 12–13), Rahner has said this about man's transcendental experience: 'In knowledge and freedom, man becomes the very essence of transcendence. That may sound rather pretentious, but it is unavoidable, and what I refer to in these terms is, in the end, the ultimate ineradicable essential structure of man . . . The movement of the mind or spirit towards the individual object with which he is concerned always aims at the particular object by passing beyond it. The individually and specifically and objectively known thing is always grasped in a broader, unnamed, implicitly present horizon of possible knowledge and possible freedom, even if the reflective mind only with difficulty and only subsequently succeeds in making this implicitly present fragment or aspect of consciousness a really specific object of consciousness, and thus objectively verbalizes it. This movement . . . is boundless. Every object of our conscious mind which we encounter in our social world and environment, as it announces itself as it were of itself, is merely a stage, a constantly new starting-point in this movement which continues into the everlasting and unnamed "before us". Whatever is given in our everyday and scientific consciousness is only a minute isle (though it may be big in one sense and may be magnified by our objectifying knowledge and action, and continuously and increasingly so) in a boundless ocean of nameless mystery, that grows and becomes all the clearer the more, and the more precisely, we express our knowing and wanting in the individual and specific instance. If we tried to set a boundary to this empty-seeming horizon of our consciousness, we would find that we had already passed through and beyond that very barrier that we sought to establish'.

Where are such experiences obtained? What are the places of such transcendental experiences? There are certain classical texts in Rahner's writings in which man's experience of God is described as taking place in his experience of himself and his world or in which his experience of the Spirit and God's grace is systematically expressed. These transcendental experiences were outlined with particular clarity by Rahner in a broadcast talk some years ago. A summary of what he said on that occasion is given below.

Special Places of Transcendental Experience
Man does not have a transcendental experience, Rahner emphasizes, simply when he speaks about it afterwards. It takes place as a very concrete everyday experience, even

though it is difficult to express verbally. It occurs anonymously and implicitly in every spiritual activity. It also takes place in a clear and more systematic form in those events in which man, who is usually involved in the individual tasks and objects of everyday life, is to some extent thrown back on himself and is no longer able to deal with everything that otherwise normally concerns him.

Man has a transcendental experience, Rahner believes, when he suddenly becomes lonely and when all the individual things in his life merge into a remote silence that is more insistent than the customary noise of everyday existence. It occurs too when he is suddenly exposed to his freedom and responsibility and experiences these as something that embraces the whole of life. He has such a transcendental experience when he cannot escape from his freedom and responsibility and cannot hope for recognition, approval, and thanks. It takes place when he is confronted with the responsibility which is silent and infinite, which exists, but is not subject to us and cannot be manipulated by us, yet is at the same time the innermost and most distinctive element in us. We are also aware of this experience, Rahner suggests, when we recognize the way in which it spreads silently throughout our whole existence, penetrating and uniting everything but remaining incomprehensible, when we learn that this responsibility is not what validly exists because we carry it out freely, but that it is precisely what makes demands on our freedom and what is still present even if we deny our responsibility and try to run away from it.

This transcendental experience is also found, according to Rahner, in personal love. Man is accepted absolutely and unconditionally in love, although he cannot, in his fragmentary and finite being, find a satisfactory reason for the absolute and unconditional character of love. He has a transcendental experience when he overcomes the other's doubts and self-questioning with incomprehensible boldness and when he trusts the absolute claim of love and traces it back to an origin that is not subject to it, but is at the same time at the heart of it and distinct from it, while remaining incomprehensible.

Man also has an experience of transcendental reality when he is silently confronted with death and apparent nothingness, accepts it voluntarily and is not destroyed, but changed by it, liberated, as it were, to the freedom that is entirely without support and is therefore unconditional. There are many other similar ways in which man is open to the incomprehensible mystery and in which he can become conscious of the fact that he is a prisoner of his own disturbing finiteness—a state that undoubtedly exists and causes cruel suffering, Rahner believes. This occurs, for example, when he ceases to be aware of the infinite and incomprehensible reality that surrounds him everywhere or when he is afraid of it because it is silently and pervasively present in everything and yet not fully at his disposal.

In this context too, Rahner points out, it is possible to speak of the joy, the faithfulness, the ultimate fear, and the longing that make such great demands, the disturbing experience of relentless truth that is always there, even though it may be mocked or denied, the serene peace that does not defend every individual matter absolutely and for this reason gains everything, the experience of beauty, the promise of what is still to come, the experience of radical and inescapable guilt that can nonetheless be quickly and incomprehensibly forgiven, the experience of the validity of what has apparently passed, but which has really become and is, and, finally, the experience of the unending openness of the future that is pure promise.

Rahner stresses the importance of a very concrete assessment of this transcendental experience, not by losing ourselves in a consideration of the individual aspects of the world around us, but by reflecting deeply about the density of the experience which can be found everywhere in our everyday lives, in which—to use the image which we have already quoted and which he employed in an article on man's experience of God—we live on the beach of the infinite sea of mystery, occupied with the grains of sand we find there.[17]

It should, then, be clear from Rahner's outline of the many different places of transcendental experience in human life—and it would not be difficult to add considerably to this list or to go more deeply into each of the places mentioned—that this experience is not restricted to the two fundamental human activities of knowledge and freedom. Rahner has also frequently spoken of an infinite anticipation of knowledge in the direction of absolute being and of the unlimited horizon of absolute freedom. His concentration on these fundamental activities of human spirituality has one distinct advantage: namely, that it is possible to see in them that transcendental experience is always present in every consciously spiritual act and that it is also the condition of the possibility of that human act. The disadvantage of Rahner's theory of absolute being, however, is that it is very abstract and difficult to understand. It is therefore more useful for us to consider here those particular places of transcendental experience which are easier to understand and at the same time easier to verify by our own day-to-day experience.

The A Priori *Structure of Transcendental Experience*

If these experiences are analyzed, it at once becomes clear that they are inevitable for everyone, that they are both intimately present in the life of each man and also quite different from him, that man experiences more in this experience of himself than he is (categorially) himself and finally that he accomplishes in such an experience an *a priori* transcendence that is superior to all concrete categorial experience. What has to be demonstrated here is that this categorial experience, as the condition of its possibility, requires a transcendence of the kind that is not simply the product or the sum total of experiences that have already taken place. We shall not at present ask whether this transcendence is an experience of God.

In the first place, as I have suggested, these experiences are inevitable for man. There should be no difficulty with regard to this assertion. Rahner, who describes love as a radical trust, has said that every man is questioned as to whether he can discover this experience of love in himself or whether he is trying to repress it. 'A third possibility', he goes on in his meditation *I believe in Jesus Christ,* 'which is a simple, innocent failure to have such an experience, can only be accepted in the case of a personally immature person; it hardly needs to be discussed that such people exist side by side with normal, adult citizens'. Experiences of love, freedom, responsibility, fear, and unfulfilled longing can all be had, Rahner insists, in varying degrees of intensity, but the fact remains that they are had, inevitably, by all human beings. If anyone disputes the truth, Rahner has said, he will assert it again in this particular dispute.

It is possibly more difficult to prove that what is most intimately present in man is at the same time different from him. What is not disputed here is that the transcendental experiences discussed so frequently in Rahner's writings are intimately present in man's life—this intimate presence is in fact expressed by the inevitability of these experiences. How can these experiences, however, be quite different from man, incomprehensible phenomena that can be seen as an absolute promise and infinite hope? How can they be characterized as something that is not man himself, even though man experiences it? Rahner is clearly convinced that, however much man associates with the categorial things of his environment and however much he is con-

cerned with encounters with his fellow men, he does not
simply accept these categorial contacts as purely factual data,
as an animal might. On the contrary, Rahner insists, because
of his spirituality, he always subjects these categorial things
or data to certain considerations, evaluates them in accordance with certain norms, and classifies them within a certain
sphere that is neither the result of categorial experiences
nor the sum total of those experiences, but transcends all
empirical experience and either belongs to man's *a priori*
structure or even constitutes that structure. The purely
factual, categorial datum is, in other words, simply as it is. It
cannot be evaluated as such. Nothing can be required of it.
In itself, it is neither false nor true, neither valuable nor
meaningless, neither lovable nor beautiful, and neither a
cause of hope nor a reason for despair.

Nonetheless, man is constantly evaluating. We make
assertions with the claim of truth. (Not all our assertions
contain this claim, but many do.) We question the meaning
of life, even when we feel impelled to say that it has none.
We are bored because the 'storehouse' of our life is empty
and because we transcend everything that we encounter and
look forward to greater fulfilment. We entrust ourselves to
another person in radical love. We are ourselves loved and
know that man alone, in his pure contingency, cannot make
such a claim of absolute love. We are happy and know at the
same time that that particular happiness will never be ours
in this life. We experience again and again the limits of our
existence and experience ourselves and everything in the
world as limited. At the same time, we also know that we can
only recognize what is limited as limited when we transcend
it.

I shall deal with the origin and destiny of this transcendence, as I have already said, later on. In the meantime,
however, I am bound to stress the importance in Rahner's
teaching of the fact that man, in the transcendality of his

experiences with the world, transcends these experiences on the basis of the *a priori* structure of his spirituality. Rahner is indeed so convinced of this fact that he often speaks of experiences of the absolute claim. Such an absolute claim is made by truth, human responsibility, and radical love.

Rahner regards all these as forming a single transcendental experience that can be had along two ways, the *via eminentiae* and the *via negationis*. 'Ultimately the *via eminentiae* and the *via negationis* are not two ways or two stations one behind the other on a way, but two aspects of one and the same experience', he has written in *The Spirit in the Church* (p. 18). It should be clear what this means if we recall that there are two kinds of experiences. On the one hand, there are experiences of what ought not to be. These are the experiences of the *via negationis,* the way of negation, which only exists because the positive, transcendant way is present in the background and as a horizon. On the other hand, however, there are also experiences which are positively fulfilling and promise even greater fulfilment. Man is always open to greater happiness and greater fulfilment. Rahner, as we have seen, never ceases to stress this openness of man.

To conclude this brief analysis of transcendental experiences, I should like to draw attention to two aspects. The *a priori* structure of our knowing, willing, and acting is the condition of the possibility of our knowledge, responsibility and concrete experiences and, as such, it cannot be the product or the sum total of our experiences. This is not a tautological statement. After all, our knowledge is always gained within the sphere of an apparently endless number of possibilities of knowledge and it is only in this way that one aspect of knowledge can be known and distinguished and that we can be sure that 'knowing one thing' does not necessarily mean 'knowing everything'. The same applies to the claim of truth and responsibility and to the negative experiences and expectations of fulfilment known to man.

The knowledge that something ought not to be or ought not to be as it is is something that only man can have. Man is also the only being who can transcend an experience of happiness and beauty and move towards even greater fulfilment. This is not the sum total or distillate of man's experience. It is far too uniformly present in all men for it to be that. What is more, all human experience is not sufficient for it, since, whenever concrete experience is transcended by expectation, evaluation and judgment, more is present than simply that experience itself and more is involved than simply the concrete, categorial, factual datum.

Only a radical and critical positivist would dispute this. Max Horkheimer once described this critical positivism as 'the myth of what is the case', and this is a very accurate description of it. Rahner has insisted again and again on man's expression of his own existence. In expressing his existence, he is not exclusively concerned with truths, which are only present when the 'case' is taken up (in other words, empirically verified). In this context, it is worth while remembering what Rahner has said about the inexpressible mystery—if rationalists and positivists forbid us to speak about it, saints, poets, and those who reveal the whole of man's existence will not allow themselves to be silenced.

One question, a very important one, still remains to be answered and an attempt will be made in the following chapter to find the answer on the basis of Rahner's theology. It is this: Is the *a priori* structure of man something that only exists in man's spirituality or does it correspond to an objectively existing reality that is different in essence from man—the reality that we call 'God'? In other words, is man's experience of himself really also an experience of God?

· 3 ·

God-Not an Alien Term for Man

Man's transcendental experiences occupy, as we have seen in the preceding chapter and will see when we reconsider this question later on, a central place in Rahner's thinking. A glance at Rahner's own presentation and analysis of these experiences—and no reader can fail to observe how often he himself stresses their importance in his own writings—will show that they have a 'poetic' sound and are expressed in what would now be called 'evocative' language. This is quite understandable if it is borne in mind that Rahner believes that man's experience of himself is always an experience of God and that this experience of God occurs in man's categorial experience which is, of course, his primary and immediate experience. The result of this is that the transcendental aspect of this experience (as the condition of its possibility) can easily be overlooked and concealed by the categorial experience.

Rahner is concerned with two elements when he deals with God and man's experience of God. He is in the first place concerned to show that 'God' is not a foreign term for man, but is rather simply the name given to a reality that always accompanies man's expression of his own life and has to be revealed to man and made explicitly conscious by an appeal to his own experience. Rahner, however, also knows, of course, that the transcendental aspect—man's experience of God in his experience of himself—can also, precisely because it is not a categorial experience, be differently interpreted, repressed, or even denied. This may happen for reasons to which no guilt can be attributed. Rahner has therefore been faced with the task of explaining man's transcendental experiences in such a way that they can function as a proof of the existence of God. This task, moreover, presents itself in such a way that man cannot or should not, on the one hand, be told from outside who God is, because God is, as it were, only the name for man's transcendental experience. On the other hand, the identity of man's transcendental experience and his experience of God has also to be established, because it is not enough simply to call any human experience an experience of God. What man experiences has to be rationally justified in reflection about that experience as an experience of God.

What does this mean in real terms? It means that, in any case of finding evidence for the existence of God, man's transcendental experience must be seen as a real reference to an objectively existing reality that is absolute, infinite, and unlimited, a reality that cannot be questioned as a fulfilment of man's being, but in fact constitutes the condition of the possibility of the availability of the world and man. What is absolute is the mode of being that, in its being and its properties, is not related to anything else, but in fact exists on its own and is its own fulfilment, having, in other words, value, truth, meaning, and so on of its own and not in relation to another or derived from another. God is a reality which exists independently of man and in this sense objectively and is essentially different in quality from man and his world. Rahner therefore sees it as part of the task, in proving the existence of God, to demonstrate that this reality (as the condition of the possibility of man's expression of his own spiritual existence) exists as such. In carrying out this task, Rahner is conscious that the various proofs of the existence of God taken as a whole are no more than special forms of the one fundamental transcendental experience of man.[18]

In connection with the traditional proofs of the existence of God, Rahner has said that, on the one hand, they were presented as though their aim was to prove something to man of which he had never heard. God and man's knowledge of God were treated as something brought to man from a long way off, like news of life in a distant country which no one had ever visited. On the other hand, Rahner also stresses, these proofs of the existence of God were furthermore presented by people who, because of their personal lives and above all the environment in which they lived, had never been disturbed by the slightest doubt about the existence of God.

What, then, do we need today to replace these earlier proofs? Rahner has suggested an 'initiation' into the original experience of God. This, he thinks, is necessary because modern man living in a secular society tends towards atheism and has a decidedly positivistic and pragmatic attitude which is far removed from the experience of God and from the type of reflection that is presupposed without question in the traditional proofs of the existence of God.

Proof of the Existence of God and the Atheistic Criticism of Religion

Rahner's treatment of the arguments used by the atheistic criticism of religion is sporadic rather than systematic, but it is still possible to draw certain conclusions with regard to his response to the atheism or the various forms of atheism found in the twentieth century. Before I do this, however, I must examine the arguments of atheism itself, at least in broad outline, and look at the fundamental postulates of the criticism of religion.

To do this, I have to begin with the philosophy of Kant and consider the possibility of metaphysics or, to be more precise, metaphysics of knowledge. Kant did not dispute the existence of God, but he did dispute the possibility of man's knowledge transcending the world (that is, the world of experience) in such a way that a philosophical knowledge of God could be reached. Rahner would express this idea in the following way: the categorial world is the limit of my knowledge—an idea that was taken up in a fundamental way by the critical rationalists. Man is only able to know what is finite. He cannot know what is infinite. Man is, in his possibility of knowing, a prisoner in his finite nature and the conceptions characterized by Kant as ideas (God—man—world) only act as an incentive to man's restlessness to escape from his limited world of experience, although he cannot do that in his theoretical knowledge.

Hegel, however, recognized that it was not possible to know a limitation simply as a limitation without having transcended this limitation in one way or another. I cannot know either a single object or a sum total of objects as limited if there is simply nothing more beyond or behind these objects or the sum total of them. A knowledge that knows its limitations has already transcended itself.

Rahner makes use of this idea to a considerable extent, as a result of his study of Joseph Maréchal's transcendental philosophy. It is also confirmed by human experience that we know ourselves to be finite and limited as human beings. Rahner has asked more than once about the condition of the possibility for our knowing what is limited as limited and what is finite as finite. Kant was too exclusively preoccupied with our knowledge of things;[19] Rahner, on the contrary, is concerned with the possibility of finite knowledge as finite and with what must be given in the knowing subject *a priori* so that he may know what he knows and how he knows it.

Rahner's fundamental argument therefore takes the following form. A finite system such as man cannot know itself as finite if it were nothing more than a finite system. In this context, Rahner points to the animal, that has no knowledge of its finite nature, or to the human organ of hearing, for example, which does not 'know' that there are, in addition to the sounds that it hears, other, ultrasonic waves that it cannot hear. Man, however, is able, as a spiritual being, to know what is finite as such and is also able to recognize himself as finite and limited, in other words, as a 'case of being'. According to Rahner, man is, despite the finite character of his system, always confronted with himself as a whole. He is able to call everything into question. He can also always question everything that can be expressed individually in anticipation of everything. By presupposing the possibility of a purely finite horizon of questioning, he transcends that possibility and demonstrates that he is a being of infinite horizon. By experiencing his finite nature, Rahner insists, he experiences himself as a transcendent being or spirit. The infinite horizon of human questioning is experienced as a horizon which continues to recede the more answers man is able to give himself.

If, then, man is able to go beyond the empirical world in his knowledge—at least in the form of a question—then he cannot accept what is finite and empirical as the ultimate limit of his possibility of knowledge, because, by knowing an individual as finite or the sum total of all finite natures as limited, he has already gone beyond this in anticipation of all being. It is true, Rahner has said, that this anticipation does not present God directly as an object to man's spirit, because the anticipation does not present, of its own accord, any object in itself as the condition of the possibility of objective knowledge.[20] But in this anticipation, as a necessary and already achieved condition of human knowledge and of all human action, there is a consent to the existence of an absolute being, that is, God.

Is this really the case? Can only a being which is absolute know what is limited as limited? The situation can certainly be different in the case of a comparative contrast between what is limited. I can know, for example, that a squirrel is not a symphony by Beethoven, which is the same as saying that Rahner does not want to dispute the fact *that* what is limited is limited or that I, as a person, have my limitations and that death is the ultimate limit of my life (or at least of my life on earth). Anticipation of absolute being, which cannot therefore be marked off from other being, does not put an end to the finite nature of what is finite, nor does it imply that what is finite is anything other than finite. The fact that I cannot fly without the help of some mechanical means does not mean that there must be beings who can fly. What it does mean is that my limits are not everything or rather, that I am not everything and that knowledge is only possible if I, aware of my finite nature, transcend it.[21]

This, however, once again raises the question: Can the anticipation only be of something finite? Rahner asks this question and replies: Anticipation of something that is relatively unlimited is contradictory. The contradiction, he insists, is not to be found in the content of concepts themselves, as though the totality of the objects of man's knowledge on the one hand and the concept of finiteness itself on the other contained a mutual contradiction. On the contrary, the contradiction exists, according to Rahner, between the postulation of this assumption and its content. Knowledge of the inner finiteness of the totality of the objects of man's knowledge calls for an anticipation which goes beyond this finiteness, with the result that this inner finiteness may be not simply factually present, but also possible to be grasped as such.

As the condition of the possibility of finite knowledge, there has to be an anticipation of infinite being, because it is only when confronted with this infinite horizon that it is possible to know and grasp what is finite in its finiteness and limited nature, whether it is individually finite or the totality of all finite things. Rahner regards knowledge of the finiteness of what is finite as something that cannot be brought about by nothing, since nothing can only bring about nothing and cannot make what is finite known as something finite. The same can also be said of freedom and might lead to an absolute value as the condition of the possibility of human freedom, thus enabling the categorial values of this world to be experienced as limited values and making a full freedom of choice possible. We may summarize this idea by saying that to experience a limit as a limit—whether we see it as the possibility of knowledge or as a possible object of freedom of choice—contains much more than the pure availability or presence of a limit.

This also applies to human judgment. (It was Maréchal who first took these reflections a stage further to consider the question of judgment.) Kant insisted that his statement that the empirical world was the limit of human knowledge was a true statement, not only for man, but also for all spiritual beings. He was also obliged to admit that the statement that human knowledge is restricted to empirical knowledge cannot be a knowledge gained simply from empirical experience. We do not need to, nor are we able to deal with this question here. What is important is the insight that knowledge of the finite nature of what is finite is only possible if something infinite is also known at the same time, something with which the finite element stands in contrast. What is finite and can be known as finite cannot, as the condition of this possibility, be finite and also be the sum total of all finite natures and continue to be finite, with the result that, in man's transcendental experience, the unlimited, infinite being is at the same time experienced and, what is more, it is experienced as the condition of the possibility of human knowledge and freedom and not as what man is in himself.

Atheism did not, however, cease to develop with the death of Kant. The infinite aspect of man's nature, derived from Hegel, was taken up by Feuerbach, who interpreted this infinite quality as applying exclusively to man's consciousness, with the result that God can be seen as man's infinite consciousness and thought of erroneously as objectively existing, whereas in fact God does not really exist, but is a projection of man's own infinite consciousness whenever man believes in God. God, in other words, is no more than the infinite nature of man himself falsely and erroneously objectivized outwards in man's thoughts.

A fairly firm model for atheism has, in fact, become established over the years. It is that man is able to transcend the data of his environment and is never entirely satisfied with what simply is. In the dynamic thrust of his spirit, he is always looking beyond himself to something more, a fulfilment, but this only exists, as it were, in his head, as an idea or a wish. It is not an objectively existing reality. In other words, it is not God.

We cannot discuss here the reasons given by the critics of religion to explain the fact that man erroneously believes in God. It is accepted almost unquestioningly by these critics that the existence of God is simply a product of man's imagination and a projection of a human wish. Roger Garaudy, a Marxist philosopher, has said that even the name of God is rejected because it implies a present reality, whereas the Marxist only experiences a demand and that infinity is for the Marxist an absence and a demand, while it is a presence and a promise for the Christian.[22]

There are many different forms of atheism in the West, but they are all based on the conviction that man's ability to transcend himself and the categorial world, as Rahner calls it, is no more than a subjective ability, in other words, an idea, demand, wish, or illusion present in his mind and not corresponding to any objective reality, with the result that he is bound to remain, in his ability to know, within the realm of the finite and also that nothing but the finite exists. What the atheist cannot accept is that the so-called infinite nature of the human spirit is an infinite quality that is essentially different from him and his world, since this at once gives rise to the question as to where man's infinite consciousness, as understood in this way, can come from and how he, as a finite, limited being, is able to have a consciousness that contradicts his finite nature.

Whether the infinite aspect of man is regarded as an absence and a demand (Garaudy) or whether God is simply thought of as the projection of man's wishes and therefore as objectively nothing (nihilism), the critics of religion do not think of infinity as something that is essentially different from man and his world, but as something that is intimately related to man's ideas and wishes, which are, in their view, ultimately finite. In concrete terms, this means that, for an atheist, everything is finite, since the sum total of all finite natures is finite or, to express this idea differently, the progress to infinity does not bestow a qualitatively different mode of being on what is finite. For an atheist, then, everything is finite and limited, at least in the sense that an infinity of the kind recognized for God by the believer is excluded.

We can only work out Rahner's reply to these critics of religion from what he has said in various comments at different times, since he has not dealt systematically with their arguments. In the first place, however, it is clear from his observations that he believes that the atheists' assertion—and therefore, by implication, the materialists' claim—that everything is limited and material has no particular meaning. If a materialist asserts that there is only matter, he has said, we should ask him what he means by matter in his claim that it is the only reality and we would learn from this that the first and last statement of the whole materialistic system has no particular meaning, since there can, by definition, be nothing on the basis of which this whole system can be determined.

In the same way, the conviction is expressed by the atheistic critics of religion that everything is finite and even meaningless, since there is nothing with which this 'everything' can be contrasted, and since it forms part of the characteristic of all statements about this 'everything' that it cannot be set off against anything else that does not exist. The word 'finite' would, after all, lose all meaning because it is combined in this context with 'everything'. The statement 'everything is finite' can only mean that man is convinced that he is always confronted only with what is finite. In that case, then, he has to be satisfied with the question asked above, that is, how he can know everything that is finite as finite and whether this assertion that everything is finite is not simply an *a priori* structure of his ability and that it does not, for this reason, represent an authentic statement about everything. On the other hand, if the assertion that everything is finite is in the long run simply the fact of experience that I am always confronted only with what is finite, then this cannot be disputed. The question is only concerned with the possibility of experiences of finiteness, not with the factual nature of those experiences.

In the second place, Rahner has asked on the same basis whether what is finite should itself be the condition of the possibility of man's experiences of finiteness. Surely this amounts to trying to pull oneself out of the bog by one's own hair? What, after all, is implied in this atheistic assertion? It can only be that what is finite is itself the condition of the possibility for the fact that nothing that is finite can fill and satisfy the dynamism of my spirit and that nothing finite can justify the claim that truth, responsibility, love, and faithfulness are absolute.

The essence of transcendental experience, as we have already seen, is, after all, that man—and only man—can know that something negative is something that ought not to be. Only man is able to experience the limited happiness and the limited fulfilment of his own world as a fragmentary promise of a greater fulfilment. Only he can respond to the claim of truth and responsibility made by his freedom in an absolute way and do this, moreover, primarily in personal encounter.

Should these experiences not, however, at the same time be made possible by what is finite, limited and contingent and not by what is necessarily absolute? There is no reason why what is in itself finite should be transcended and even if I do not know the quantitative totality of all finite being, nothing finite, not even its totality, is sufficient to explain why everything finite leaves me unfulfilled.

Assuming that man is capable, in his thinking, of transcendence, which is, of course, something that even an atheist would not dispute, we are bound to conclude that this ability to transcend what is finite cannot be based on finite man himself or his finite power of imagination. We can, for example, ask with Rahner: Can a finite system know its finiteness? Can he know his finiteness as such if what lies behind this finiteness is only finiteness or even nothing at all? Can he experience all forms of happiness in this world and remain unfulfilled by them if these forms of worldly happiness are not experienced against the unsystematic background of a fulfilment that is really complete? Can he claim the right of absolute validity for himself or others if human dignity and human rights do not participate in an absolute value? Freud was to some extent mistaken in describing religion as an illusion. He was right, of course, when he said that a human wish does not guarantee the fulfilment of what is desired. A peasant girl can certainly have the illusion that a prince will come and woo her, but, as Freud insisted, 'it is not very probable'.

There can be no doubt that Freud was right here, but the fact that he equated religion with a belief motivated above all by aspiration or wish shows that he was not considering the fundamental problem itself. We are, after all, not primarily concerned in this case with whether God is a human wish or aspiration, but with the condition of the possibility of the fact—to pursue the image provided by Freud himself—that a prince is not the complete fulfilment of a peasant girl and that the girl, even if she has her prince, always has something new in the storehouse of her consciousness, such as expectations of happiness, with the result that this storehouse always remains empty. God cannot be dispensed with as easily as that, and simply called a wish-structure of the human imagination or the attempt of man to transcend his own finite nature through the power of imagination.

Finally, there is a third possibility open to atheists: that is, to dismiss all these ideas as uninteresting fancies and in this way to provide human life as a whole with the stamp of ultimate meaninglessness. It is important in this context to bear in mind that no one can be compelled to reflect upon his transcendental experiences and that no one can be prevented from situating the ultimate point of his questioning and seeking in the finite nature of the world and from regarding that factual, secular sphere with its inner laws and man himself in his factual structure as the ultimate data, which can provide no further explanation. Rahner has commented in this context: 'I would not maintain here that it is possible to take any drugs against the pain caused by the fact that transcendentality cannot be fulfilled. This unfulfilled transcendentality continues even if it is repressed. It is active in countless phenomena in individual and collective life. It is present, for example, in the boredom that swallows up everything that is concrete and colourful in a grey mist. It can also be found in our aggression against the present, which strikes us as so imperfect and unbearable that we try to escape from it into a utopian and unreal future. Our attempts to seek flight from a world that seems to be too narrow and lacking in comfort also point to this unfulfilled transcendentality, which is also present in the attempt to transcend what is finitely pleasant or meaningful in an elaborate pleasure or an ideology and to do this in such a way that the phenomenon of finiteness in all these transcended realities is no longer experienced'(*Christian at the Crossroads*).

What can we say in conclusion? It is that the condition of the possibility of these transcendental experiences can only be a reality that is given *in* man as the presupposition of his expression of his own existence. It is, however, as what is infinite, unlimited, nameless, and absolute, not man himself, with the result that man is, in a very real sense, 'more' than he is. The infinite nature of man's consciousness is, of course, to be found in man's thinking, but it is not to be found exclusively in his thinking processes. Because he is not the infinite, but experiences himself in many different ways as infinite, he cannot be identified with it. This infinite element, however, really exists and is independent of man, because the reality of his transcendental experiences calls for an equally real, objectively existing condition of its possibility. If, in other words, my transcendental experiences are real, then the condition of their possibility is also real, because the first cannot exist without the second.

Speaking about God

It ought to be clear from what has been said so far, especially in the sections dealing with philosophy, that Rahner's way of speaking about God is marked by a certain vagueness. This vagueness can be explained by the fact that the concrete place where man's experience of himself is also his experience of God is at the same time his experience that is transcendental and based on categorial objects and that his reflection about the transcendentality of this experience does not, in Rahner's view, bring about that experience, but is precisely a later reflection about it.

This necessarily results in a dilemma—on the one hand, we have to speak about our experience of what is infinite, unlimited, nameless, and absolute and, on the other, we know that anything that we say about it is a falsification of our original experience. Rahner himself has said that we are constantly trying to name our transcendental experience, but can only call it by such names as nameless, unlimited, or infinite, because, in selecting a particular name from among many, we at once restrict or distinguish the experience. Conversely, he has also pointed out that the condition of distinguishing by giving a name cannot really have a name because, as the condition of the possibility of all categorial distinction, it cannot itself be marked off from other experience by the same means of distinction. Every name that we give to God—including the name 'God'—is no more than a means for enabling us to reflect rationally, and for this reason Rahner's frequently complicated way of expressing himself when he speaks about God is clearly necessary because the 'everything' cannot be marked off from anything else. He speaks, for example, of a direction followed by our transcendental experience, not because he wants to express himself in a strange and complicated way, but because, if he were to speak of God, he might, he believes, give rise to the serious misunderstanding that he was speaking of God in terms of an objectivized conceptuality, whereas his intention is to show that 'God' is already given by transcendence and is present in advance in that transcendence.

For the same reason, Rahner's statements about God vary. They vary, to be more precise, between positive and negative formulations and expressions. In his terminology, then, God is called the infinite horizon, the fulness of being, the ground of all hope, the unlimited distance, the sacred or holy mystery, love, faithfulness, and truth. God is also, according to Rahner, the silent rule over us, existing in his own mode of presence and absence. The direction of our transcendence is given to us, Rahner believes, in the mode of silence, renunciation, and distance. Our experience of God is an experience of emptiness and darkness. It leads into the dark deserted abyss known as God.

Rahner is also aware of man's existential experience of the apparent meaninglessness of life. He gives two reasons for this. In the first place, it is a fact that man is oriented towards the inexpressible mystery, but because he is not himself that mystery and also because he has no power over it, the question as to whether or not human life is meaningful is ultimately a question of how that mystery—God—is related to man and whether God accepts man or thrusts him out into the darkness of meaninglessness. Positive acceptance by God can only be hoped for at the philosophical level of thought, but it cannot be proved. The result of this, Rahner insists, is that everything—and this means really everything—depends on a divine revelation. Man is therefore a hearer of God's word, hoping—without in fact knowing—that this word will not be ultimate rejection. It is for this reason that the heart of Christian faith is, in

Rahner's opinion, very simple—in his *Christian at the Cross-roads*, he describes it 'knowing that one is accepted by God in Jesus Christ'.

In the second place, Rahner believes that our experience of the apparent meaninglessness of human life is based on the fact that faith in God does not in any way solve the riddle of that life and, what is more, cannot solve it. Rahner does not, in other words, share the opinion of certain Christians who think that human life is made clear and transparent by faith in God and Jesus Christ. In *Christian at the Crossroads*, he says: 'My Christianity is therefore an act in which I allow myself to be released into the incomprehensible mystery and is consequently in no sense an explanation of the world or my own existence. It is rather an act in which I am prevented from regarding any experience or any understanding of reality, however good or illuminating it may be, as definitive or as entirely intelligible in itself. As a Christian, I am even less able than others to accept "ultimate" answers in which I am assured that the problem of human life is solved. No Christian is entitled to use God as one of the clear items in his life' and is, for this reason, 'the most radical of all sceptics'.

Why is this? It is because a Christian—if he really believes in the incomprehensible nature of God—cannot accept any single, individual truth as the ultimate answer to his questioning. Every individual question leads ultimately to the unanswerable question of God. 'The Christian is therefore someone who has the maddening experience of being unable to regard any opinion as quite right or any opinion as quite wrong' (*Christians at the Crossroads*). Rahner's main criticism of nihilists is that they do not treat the meaninglessness of life as something that can be understood and penetrated, when it is, on the contrary, important to leave what is not and perhaps never can be understood open, and therefore to face the world with the serenity only possible for those who understand that what cannot be changed is a holy mystery.

Rahner has pointed explicitly to the fact that man's created state is not simply an isolated case of a relationship of cause and effect. He in fact experiences himself in his transcendental experience as given the power by God to express himself spiritually. God is therefore the condition of the possibility of man's humanity and therefore, in this sense, the 'cause' of man. To understand himself as created by God and therefore in his state as a creature, he has to orient himself towards the metaphysical causal principle, as Rahner calls it, in other words, towards God as the creator of the world. Man is in this sense not a cause of the kind that is known to us in our understanding of the categorial causality of the world. He is rather the transcendental reason which constitutes a lasting and ever present process and which does not simply point back to that earlier time when creation took place. On the contrary, Rahner is convinced that creation is always taking place. I shall now consider this concept.

God's Transcendental Activity in the World

In the preceding section, the existence of God was considered primarily as static. This, of course, is inevitable in any attempt to prove the existence of God as the condition of the possibility of human knowledge. There must be something absolute, unlimited and nameless; in other words, there must be a holy mystery which makes it possible for man's spirit to be dynamic and is therefore in man, although man is not himself that infinite mystery. The infinite reality, then, which we call God gives man the power to express his spirituality and is at the same time quite different from man. This relationship is characterized by immanence and transcendence. God is intimately present in me; and he is also, at the same time, that which transcends all understanding because he cannot be contained in concepts.

If, then, we try to prove the existence of God on the basis of man's transcendental experiences, we may give the nowadays very widespread impression that God is a static pole in man's existence that is present, but inactive. Natural scientists have for a very long time tended to claim that everything—or at least almost everything—in the world can be traced back to causes within the world. There is consequently no need to regard God any more as filling in the gaps in those places where we as yet lack understanding. Another direct consequence of the progress of the natural sciences has, of course, been the spread of deism and, although this movement is no longer theologically important, it has certainly had a lasting effect, either explicitly or implicitly, on the thinking of modern man.

According to the deists, God created the world, but, having created it, left it entirely to its own immanent laws. God does not, the deists believe, intervene in his creation. The world follows rules that were given to it by God at creation. There seems to be nothing that can point tangibly to God's continued activity in the world. Everything takes place in accordance with the monotonous regularity of the world's laws.

Christian theologians have, of course, rejected this deistic teaching, but have at the same time stressed that God is only active in the world by means of second causes, in other words, causes within the world, since, if he were to intervene tangibly and verifiably in the events of the world, he would be placing himself at the level of creation. He would in this way be a categorial cause and no longer the God who is beyond this world. It is, however, precisely this fact, that there is no tangible evidence of the activity of God in the world and that, if we leave the problem of miracles out of account, there is nothing that points unambiguously to the activity of God and can be proved to be divine activity, that condemns God and faith in God to the position of a meaningless factor for the practical and religious life of man today, a factor, moreover, that has never been really known in the past and has never been regarded as possible. A God who does nothing and who, at least in the opinion of most men today, lets the world run its own course without intervening cannot have any special meaning for human life. Finally, it is not a very great step from a God whose activity cannot be experienced in the world to a God who does not exist, from a God who is not useful for any purpose in the world to a forgotten God, and finally from a forgotten God to a God who gives rise to doubt rather than faith.

Evolution and Self-Transcendence

This brief impression is accentuated by the fact of evolution. Higher life evolves in a continuous process from lower life and, in the light of this knowledge, it is easy for modern man, especially if he is less gifted metaphysically, to have the impression that the last bastion of any evidence for the existence of God has fallen. What had to be explained in the past simply by God's creation—the juxtaposition of different forms of life and different objects—can now be explained by evolution. Rahner does not doubt the fact of evolution and this acceptance has even sparked off a series of questions that are typical of his own way of thinking. He may even be the first theologian to have asked these questions that have arisen from the problem of evolution and have presented themselves to Christians in their full theological implications. The most seriously challenging ones are, of course, whether evolution means the end of faith in creation and whether it means the end of God's activity in the world.

The Church teaches and always has taught that God created the human soul, and that this is a direct act of creation. How, then, should we interpret this in the light of our present knowledge that man is the product of evolution? Can we as Christians continue to insist that only the human body has developed as a result of the evolutionary process and not the human soul or spirit? In the coming about of man, can we say that material presuppositions only apply to the direct creation of the soul?[23]

These and similar questions have been asked by Rahner and they have led to a re-appraisal of the relationship between matter and spirit and above all to a new concept, that of 'man's active transcendence of himself' as a created reality. This concept has been developed most fully by Rahner in his Christological teaching, but he has a great deal to say about it elsewhere, for example, in those parts of his theology where he deals with man as a created being 'producing' more than can be explained by causes within this world alone.

Because the concept of active transcendence of oneself is not easy to understand, it is probably better to return to our point of departure and to ask whether the evolutionary process can be explained only on the basis of our knowledge of the natural sciences, or whether an ultimate explanation of this process does not have to be found in a transcendental activity on God's part—one which should not be understood as a second cause within the sphere of what is accessible to the natural sciences, but as something that makes these second causes possible and allows the evolutionary process to take place.

Let me try to go over the ground covered by Rahner and understand what he means by the concept of man's active transcendence of himself. First, he has devoted numerous studies to a re-assessment of the relationship between matter and spirit. Second, he has attempted to draw attention to God's constant activity in his creation, especially in the datum of becoming, which confronts the natural scientist, who aims to be more than simply a natural scientist, with an apparently insoluble dilemma. This dilemma ceases in fact to be a dilemma as soon as we follow Rahner's idea of an active self-transcendence, an idea which appears to contain a contradiction when it is examined more closely.

Rahner regards it as a philosophical and theological matter of course that the relationship between spirit and matter can only be resolved dialectically. For him spirit is essentially different from matter, but, because both matter and spirit are created by God, the difference between them cannot be an absolute one. Rahner himself has stressed that matter cannot be spiritualized in an idealistic way. It is, in his opinion, wrong to see them side by side as two disparate objects of our individual experience, and a Christian is able to be a materialist and a spiritualist at the same time since all that is meant by these two words is that spirit and matter are not words for juxtaposed individual regions of the total reality, but two essentially different, but constitutive aspects of the same reality that are in every respect closely related to each other, at whatever point we encounter them. There is, then, a close affinity and an inseparable unity between matter on the one hand and spirit on the other and, as a result of this, the possibility exists that matter may become spirit, so long as the way remains open and this question represents the real problem.

In this context, Rahner himself has said that we can only make progress in our understanding of this question and arrive at a positive answer subject to certain presuppositions and conceptual conditions, if we examine the concept of active self-transcendence. There is becoming, and this becoming is ultimately not only a combination of fundamental static elements which has been spatially, temporally, and quantitatively changed, but a becoming of a really new kind which has its origin in this world and yet is not simply the same as that from which it is derived. Becoming, then, is always and essentially a transcendence of itself, not simply a replica of the same thing. Rahner has defined this becoming as the active element's transcendence of itself, brought about by the lower element itself, in brief, an 'active self-transcendence'.

The first point to bear in mind, then, is the fact of becoming and that there is a becoming from which something new emerges. This new element is not simply a combination or a re-organization of already existing basic elements or component parts, but something that was not there previously in that particular form. What comes about is a plus or something more. Rahner has called it an increase in being that is not simply a being that is different from the previous being. If it were just the second, there would have been no process of becoming, since, as Rahner has said, if there is this process of becoming, it cannot be understood in its true form as a becoming different, in which a reality becomes different, but not more. This becoming must, Rahner insists, be understood as a becoming more, as the coming about of more reality and as the effected achievement of a greater fulness of being. But does this really exist? Is this becoming and what has in fact become in the process of becoming really more than simply a combination of the earlier basic elements that were already present? Is this true at least whenever something really new emerges or has emerged?

Rahner recognizes the possibility that something can simply become different without any real increase in being,[24] but believes that this question of the mechanics of evolution lies within the province of the natural sciences, the task of which is to explain the conditions of a material kind governing the emergence of anything that is biologically new. This aspect of the process of becoming can only be dealt with by the natural sciences since the functional connection of different phenomena is precisely the task of those sciences. This can be expressed more simply: The

natural sciences are subject to the principle of the relationship between cause and effect. They provide a genetical
explanation of phenomena by discovering the scientific
genesis, in other words, the origin or causes, of those
phenomena and deducing what has become from the
genesis and explaining it in terms of this world. The task of
the natural sciences is therefore to explain a certain being
genetically on the basis of causes within this world. No more
and no less than this is done by the natural sciences and the
success achieved by them in this sphere justifies the method.
Any attempt on the part of scientists to explain the emergence of something new can therefore only be made with
reference to a spatial, temporal, or quantitative change or
combination of what already exists. This is the only way in
which the natural sciences can proceed. They can only
achieve their end by faithfully following their own methods;
and these methods can be summarized in the most general
way by saying that there must be empirically verifiable
causes within this world for everything that happens within
it, and for everything that becomes within it.

The question still remains, however, as to whether this
scientific method can explain every phenomenon. We are, in
other words, confronted by the dilemma mentioned above,
in which the natural sciences are placed if they aim to be
more than simply natural sciences and attempt to explain
the whole of the world of evolutionary becoming. Rahner
has expressed this dilemma in the following way. The
modern world-view, he has said, spoils its own fundamental
concept to a very great extent—and by this Rahner, of
course, means the concept of the world of evolutionary
becoming—by attempting to interpret what appears as new
in the history of nature and the spirit simply as the
fortuitous variation or combination of basic elements that
are already present. Even highly contemporary world-views
are, in Rahner's opinion, based on the fundamental misun-

derstanding that a radically new phenomenon that is qualitatively different and higher cannot be the product of evolution from below (if this did not therefore really exist) and that the real evolutionary process from below does not really produce anything new, but only what is quantitatively more complex. Anyone, however, whether he is a Christian, a philosopher or a natural scientist, Rahner has pointed out, who accepts the world of evolutionary becoming without prejudice simply as it is, and anyone who does not deny that something authentically new can exist in time (that there can be a real connection in time, and that it is possible for evolution to take place from below to above) cannot in the long run avoid the concept of becoming as an authentic self-transcendence. All created being, Rahner stresses, is a being that is becoming, but all becoming that really deserves the name of becoming is a becoming of the qualitatively higher that is nonetheless the act of the lower.

We can therefore say of Rahner that, in his view, it is only at the level of categorial causality that can be verified by the natural scientific method that evolution has either to be kept within the confines of material mechanism, with the result that the distinction between spirit and matter cannot be explained, or is placed outside the sphere of human understanding and has simply to be accepted as an inexplicable datum. It is not possible to escape from this dilemma. One can, on the one hand, be a materialistic mechanist, in which case one's philosophical standpoint is one that has been almost entirely abandoned by natural scientists and even by dialectical materialists. The same stones are used for building, but the new building that has emerged in the process of evolutionary becoming with these stones is something higher and more and something that is qualitatively different, in other words, an increase in being. On the other hand, however, one can believe in ultimate meaninglessness, but this has the disadvantage that it does not satisfactorily explain what exists, but it does, as something that exists, require an explanation. There still remains, in conclusion, the question: How can something higher come to be from something lower?

The explanation provided for this by the natural sciences is clearly insufficient, and I am bound to consider another point before attempting to look for an answer to this question. Since this point is philosophical, it may not be accepted by everyone and it is certainly not easy to understand. Even in traditional philosophical terms, becoming is presented in such a way that a cause that is external to what is becoming adds something to what is becoming, with the result that what is new and higher does not become new and higher of its own accord, but only because of a cause that operates from outside. This, however, means, Rahner has pointed out, that nothing in the world is in itself active and that everything is fundamentally passive. All self-motivated activity is no more than apparent. But, Rahner goes on, this contradicts all man's experience of himself, since, after all, he sees himself in all his activity as the principle of that activity.[25]

Rahner has pointed out frequently that what is new cannot simply be regarded as something that is added to what is old and what has gone before. What is more, it should not be thought of, he has repeatedly said, as simply added to the previously existing reality, but, on the one hand as what has been brought about by the previously existing reality itself and on the other, as its own inner increase in being. The reason for this is clear. If this increase in being in what is new were simply added from outside, there would obviously be no evolution in the real sense of the word.

The Transcendental Activity of God which makes Self-Transcendence Possible

The question with which I have to deal in this section is, I think, fairly clear. As we have already seen, the natural sciences are able to provide a genetical explanation, but this does not explain everything. What cannot be made clear by this explanation is how a phenomenon can transcend itself in such a way that, on the one hand, it is really the cause of something new and, on the other, this new element is also (in comparison with what has gone before) higher. The question is, then: How can a being transcend itself? How can it bring about more than it apparently is itself?

If Rahner's active self-transcendence is more than simply another descriptive term for evolution, it would seem that it contains a contradiction, since, as we have seen in the preceding paragraph, it is difficult to understand how something can transcend itself. To resolve this apparent contradiction, Rahner has made use of what he calls the 'metaphysical causal principle', which does not simply refer to a cause of the kind familiar to us from the world of our experience, but rather corresponds to the transcendental reality which, as a cause, is the condition of the possibility of man's expression of his spiritual nature. As Rahner himself has said in this context, when something new really comes about and this has its origin in a cause within this world, its cause transcends itself and becomes more reality than it is and has itself. According to the metaphysical causal principle, this self-transcendence is only possible by virtue of the dynamism of absolute being, which is at the same time the innermost element of the cause within this world, and what is also absolutely different from finite, causal being.

What, then, is this metaphysical causal principle which is not simply accessible to empirical experience, but is also required as a condition of the possibility of evolution and becoming as such? What has been said above about transcendental experiences generally also applies to God's transcendental activity in the world and strictly speaking both are simply different aspects of the same reality. In any attempt to understand myself as a man in my spiritual nature, I am able to recognize that I am not exclusively concerned in my knowledge and freedom with the categorial data of my world, but that, as the condition of the possibility of this activity and these experiences, there must also be a reality which makes it possible for me to carry out this concrete activity.

This other reality is unlimited, infinite and absolute. It is, in other words, God, dwelling in me and making it possible for me to associate with the categorial world, yet essentially different from me. The metaphysical cause to which Rahner refers again and again in this context is something that cannot be understood in accordance with the model of causality within this world. It can therefore be described as a cause which cannot be categorially defined and empirically encountered, but which nonetheless enables me to bring about what is brought about. Metaphysical causality is therefore the transcendental activity of God.

The concept of causality can be seen primarily in personal experience. It is possible to understand in the light of one's own experience what is meant by this metaphysical causality. It is clear, for example, from the phenomenon of transcendental experience that I am more in every spiritually conscious activity than the categorial activity itself, that I, in other words, transcend myself and that this transcendental aspect that is present in all my spiritual activities makes the transcendental experience possible. It is therefore possible to understand the self-transcendence of a being that occurs within the evolutionary process in the light of this original knowledge of what a metaphysical cause is. This is, as Rahner says, because we have, in this concept of self-transcendence, to take both aspects, the self and the transcendence, seriously, in other words, the whole concept of transcendence of self, if the lower element is really to be seen as the cause of the higher. This, however, could not be the case if self-transcendence were not made possible by the transcendental activity of God and sustained by that activity. It is only in this way, then, that the concept of becoming in this world can be understood as an active transcendence of self.

Rahner himself has said, with reference to the question of the possibility of an increase in being brought about from below, that we can only extricate ourselves from this difficulty if we recognize that the infinite cause which contains in advance in itself all reality as a pure act belongs to the constitution of the finite cause as such, but is not an inner aspect of that cause as a being. It should be clear, Rahner believes, from the first half of this dialectical statement that the finite cause is really able to transcend itself, in other words, that its effect is more than itself, but is nonetheless set by itself and is therefore able to transcend itself. The second part of this dialectical statement makes it clear that this effect can really be a transcendence. This would not be so if the pure act which is infinite and which belongs to the constitution of the finite cause as such were an inner aspect of the finite cause itself and if the finite cause already had in itself what, in transcending itself, it had to achieve in its self-transcendence.

I propose to conclude this chapter by looking at what status and value these considerations really have in Rahner's thought and in the whole of theology today. The point of departure for all these ideas is the direct creation of the human soul by God. Rahner is only able to give his consent to this pronouncement made by the Church's teaching office within the framework of a consideration of an evolutionary view of the world and man. Man is, he accepts, entirely the product of second causes, his parents, but he also believes that what is positively contained in this is that these parents can only be entirely the cause of man insofar as they allow that new man to come about through the power of God which makes their transcendence of themselves possible. This power is contained within their activity, but it does not form a constitutive part of their being.[26]

The direct creation of the human soul by God is, for Rahner, however, only a special case in the whole of God's continuous activity in the world. I have asked several times how it is possible to be aware of God's activity and Rahner has replied by saying that the transcendentality of God's activity with relation to the world should never be seen as a merely static bearing up of the world. On the contrary, he insists, it forms the basis and motivation of this world precisely as a world that is in a constant state of becoming by transcending itself, although God's activity is not in any sense a categorial or miraculous intervention into the world.

All these considerations have an inevitable effect on various aspects of faith which can be mentioned briefly, but unfortunately not discussed in detail here. In the first place, of course, even if this might not be the intention, it may nonetheless be true that the proof of the existence of God is possibly clearer to anyone who is not a professional theologian or philosopher than Rahner's reflections about man's transcendental experiences. But, after all, anyone who is capable of being astonished is bound to ask questions about the 'miracle' of evolution, how the universe as we know it came about, what dynamic power underlies the evolutionary process and what plan is at the base of the development of life. Plessner was certainly not right when he said: 'Man is in no way deprived of human dignity by attributing his existence to blind chance or a tendency such as increasing cerebralization'.[27] We can say with confidence that blind chance, a tendency to increasing cerebralization, laws, and a purposeful development towards higher forms of life all belong to the evolutionary process, but they do not explain it completely. What is more, the concept of self-transcendence within this world also opens the way to an understanding of the idea of wonder or miracle, not as a direct intervention on God's part into the laws of the world, but rather as a particular form of self-transcendence of the created reality which operates under certain conditions and in fact always takes place whenever something new is brought about in the world, but causes great astonishment and is called a 'miracle' only if it seems extraordinary and occurs within a religious and symbolic framework.

This question is also connected with the problem of the effectiveness of prayer. Rahner has commented in this context that what he calls a 'good idea' may result in a decision that can be shown to be correct and important in its consequences in the world. Is this 'good idea' really a divine illumination? His answer is clear—he has again and again stressed that man has the right and the duty to give a natural explanation for such 'good ideas'. But he has further pointed out that this question is also open to a more subtle interpretation on the basis of man's transcendence of himself. In the first place, he has said, I can experience and accept myself as a transcendent subject oriented towards God. In the second place, I can also freely accept this world, despite the fact that all its various aspects and functions are closely interwoven, as the concrete world in which my own concrete relationship with the absolute ground of my existence, God, is historically deeply involved. When I accept both the first and the second, this 'good idea' will objectively have a precise and positive significance within this subjective and transcendental relationship with God. I shall then be able and obliged to say that this good idea is an aspect of the one world that has been set free from its ground, and an aspect of my world of subjective relationship with God, and that it was wanted by God in its positive significance, and as such is a divine illumination. Of course, Rahner adds, it is easy to object that everything can be regarded in this way as a special intervention on God's part, so long as it is assumed that I accept the concrete situation in which my life and the world are placed in such a way that it becomes a positive and concrete form of my transcendental relationship with God. But, he concludes, this objection can be countered with the question: Why should this not be so?

Finally, the idea of a self-transcendence made possible by God's transcendental activity has led Rahner to outline an understanding of the incarnation of God in Jesus Christ that is of central importance in his theological work. I shall deal with this in the following chapter.

·4·

The Heart of Rahner's Theology

So far, I have considered Rahner's theology from what could be called, in the broadest sense of the word, the philosophical point of view. Although, as we have seen, Rahner is always a theologian even when he is speculating philosophically, the aspects of his work that we have examined in the previous chapters have had no specifically Christian or theological content. His anthropological approach to theology, which he follows with the help of the transcendental method, reaches an indisputable climax in his concept of the 'supernatural existential' factor, which is, taking the breadth and multiplicity of his theological ideas into account, the central concept in his theology, since it is the same as his concept of transcendental experiences, although under a different aspect. It is hardly possible to understand his theology if this central concept is not grasped. An understanding of what he means by the 'supernatural existential' factor may not enable us to understand the whole of his theology, but it will make a great deal intelligible, certainly the most important aspects.

The word 'existential', of course, comes from Martin Heidegger and makes a distinction between the ontological definition of 'existence' (that is, man's existence of 'being there') and the categories of things that are not there in the same sense. Existence, then, is seen by Rahner as the mode in which man expresses his being there. The question of the ontological structure of man's existence points, Rahner has indicated, to an exposition of what constitutes that existence. The existential factors form the connection between these structures. Since, then, this concept of the supernatural existential factor is, as I have said, the central point of departure in Rahner's theology for the asking and answering of a whole series of questions connected with faith, I shall try, as my first and perhaps only aim, to throw some light on it in this chapter.[28]

Grace and the Supernatural Existential Factor

As we have already seen, Rahner himself regards his theology as characterized by 'transcendental anthropology'. He has said that there are grace and certain data that exist on the basis of grace as a particular and regional reality which may well be absent in the case of the sinner or the non-believer. But he has expressed the deep theological conviction that what Christians call grace is without question a reality which is given by God in a free, dynamic relationship and which is therefore supernatural. At the same time, however, he is certain that grace is also a reality that is always present at the very centre of man's existence in knowledge and freedom and in the mode of an offer which can be accepted or rejected. In fact, he insists that it is existentially present to such an extent that man is not able in any way to abandon this transcendental peculiarity of his very being. Because of this, what Rahner himself has called—and the concept has become widely known—'anonymous Christianity' exists everywhere. There is no religion of any kind in which God's grace, however suppressed it may be and however depraved its expression may be, does not reveal itself in one way or another, and finally what Rahner has entitled the 'transcendental aspect of historical revelation' is present in the world. I shall consider some of the consequences of this supernatural existential factor in the next chapter, which is devoted to this anonymous Christianity and the universal revelation of God.

Here, however, I must consider the question of grace, since Rahner himself has called this a central concern in his theological endeavours. This grace is really supernatural grace, which is no more or less than God himself dwelling at the very centre of the existence of every man. It is given, Rahner has said, in the mode of an offer. As an offer, however, it is not only a theoretical matter, in other words, external to man, but also something which, as the grace of God, determines man to such an extent in his knowledge and freedom that it even continues to determine his existence when he refuses it. This supernatural existential factor is therefore something that continues to determine man's existence and does so *a priori* and therefore transcendentally. It determines his being ontically and ontologically,[29] preceding all his decisions.

I have already considered Rahner's view of man's transcendental structure and his understanding of man as a being who can only be and do what he is and does because he always sees his categorial world in the light of a transcendental *a priori*—even if this is at first and originally only present in an unsystematic and unreflected form. This is now given a theological emphasis, and man is seen in his transcendental structure not simply as natural man, but rather as man who has been called by God to supernatural salvation. This state of being called by God—or by grace, which is God himself—forms a permanent and ontological factor which determines man's being, with the result that man's experience of himself is also an experience of God and at the same time an experience of grace and, what is more, an experience in the transcendental quality that is distinctive to man's experience of God.[30]

The Origin and Development of the Idea

In his earliest works, Rahner described man as a being who was open to God and to God's revelation in an unlimited and fundamental way. The idea of a permanent and personal decision made by each man as the result of receiving God's grace emerged a little later, but even so at quite an early stage in his writings. It first appeared in an early unpublished lecture entitled *De Gratia* and shortly afterwards in several early essays on nature and grace and the concept of uncreated grace in scholastic theology published in the first volume of his *Theological Investigations*. This idea of the relationship between nature and grace was the point of departure in Rahner's thinking for the idea of a supernatural existential factor that was increasingly developed in his later writings. I shall return to this, but feel that the best approach to the question is not to follow the development of the idea chronologically in Rahner's publications,[31] but rather to present those theological aspects of the question as a whole in which truth, necessity, and fruitfulness appear as the result of accepting a supernatural existence.

Transcendence as an Experience of Grace

Rahner speaks consciously as a Christian theologian about man's experience of God and the proofs of the existence of God. He never asks questions about these matters simply on the basis of pure philosophy. It is therefore not easy to ascertain how much trust he places in a purely philosophical proof of the existence of God. He seems to regard it as possible, but is also conscious of the fact that man's transcendental experience can also be differently interpreted, and that this can be done without any guilt or malice on the part of man.

Rahner himself describes the experience of God as an

experience of emptiness, darkness and non-understanding or as a desert experience. What is even more important in this context, however, is that, no matter how conclusive our evidence of the existence of God may be, it does not tell us the most decisive thing of all, namely whether and how God is related to man as the most decisive question in man's life. The idea of a God who denies himself to man is so strange to us because of our knowledge of the content of Christian faith that we are almost unable to accept it. But is it so much a matter of course that God should turn towards us—to me and every individual man—in grace? Is it so unquestionable that he should share the mystery of his grace with us and not be a God who rejects, denies himself to us and condemns us, thrusting us into ultimate meaninglessness from which there is no escape? Where, then, do we find those 'traces of angels' that lead us back to the conviction that everything will be well? Rahner has said in answer to this question that God's grace is at work everywhere, giving men hope and confidence, even where there is no explicit faith in the Christian revelation: 'There is God and his liberating grace. There we find what we Christians call the Holy Spirit of God. Then we experience something which is inescapable (even when suppressed) in life, and which is offered to our freedom with the question whether we want to accept or whether we want to shut ourselves up in a hell of freedom by trying to barricade ourselves against it' (*The Spirit in the Church,* p.22).

I have already pointed out, when I was discussing Rahner's concept of man's transcendental experience, that he has provided the best descriptions of such experiences in his accounts of man's experiences of God or the Spirit, in which he has appealed to man's experience of himself and has drawn attention to the condition of the possibility of such experiences. In this context, then, I would like to quote one of Rahner's finest texts, in which he makes it clear that man's transcendental experiences, heightened by his super-

natural existential experience, are also experiences of grace
and therefore experiences of the Holy Spirit. Within this
framework, then, it is possible for Rahner to ask where and
how man has these experiences of the Spirit. Our experience of God is present in our various experiences of the
Spirit, which makes it possible for us to experience God and
form the horizon of that experience and the condition of its
possibility. The following passage from *The Spirit in the
Church* (pp. 18–22) is entitled 'Experiencing the Spirit in
Actual Life':

'I can now refer to the actual life-experiences which,
whether we come to know them reflectively or not, are
experiences of the Spirit. It is important that we experience
them in the right way. In the case of these indications of the
actual experience of the Spirit in the midst of banal
everyday life, it can no longer be a question of analyzing
them individually right down to their ultimate depth—
which is the Spirit. And no attempt can be made to make a
systematic tabular summary of such experiences. Only
arbitrarily and unsystematically selected examples are possible.

Let us, for instance, take someone who is dissatisfied with
his life, who cannot make the good will, errors, guilt and
fatalities of his life fit together, even when, as often seems
impossible, he adds remorse to this accounting. He cannot
see how he is to include God as an entry into the accounting,
as one that makes the debit and the credit, the notional and
the actual values, come out right. This man surrenders
himself to God or—both more imprecisely and more
precisely—to the hope of an incalculable ultimate reconciliation of his existence in which he whom we call God dwells;
he releases his unresolved and uncalculated existence, he
lets go in trust and hope and does not know how this miracle
occurs that he cannot himself enjoy and possess as his own
self-actuated possession.

There is a man who discovers that he can forgive though he receives no reward for it, and silent forgiveness from the other side is taken as self-evident.

There is one who tries to love God although no response of love seems to come from God's silent inconceivability, although no wave of emotive wonder any longer supports him, although he can no longer confuse himself and his life-force with God; although he thinks he will die from such a love, because it seems like death and absolute denial; because with such a love one appears to call into the void and the completely unheard-of; because this love seems like a ghastly leap into groundless space; because everything seems untenable and apparently meaningless.

There is one man who does his duty where it can apparently only be done, with the terrible feeling that he is denying himself and doing something ludicrous which no one will thank him for.

There is a man who is really good to another man from whom no echo of understanding and thankfulness is heard in return, whose goodness is not even repaid by the feeling of having been 'selfless', noble and so on.

There is one who is silent although he could defend himself, although he is unjustly treated, who keeps silence without feeling that his silence is his sovereign unimpeachability.

There is a man who obeys not because he must and would otherwise find it inconvenient to disobey, but purely on account of that mysterious, silent and inconceivable thing that we call God and the will of God.

There is a man who renounces something without thanks or recognition, and even without a feeling of inner satisfaction.

There is a man who is absolutely lonely, who finds all the right elements of life pale shadows; for whom all trustworthy handholds take him into the infinite distance, and who does not run away from this loneliness but treats it with ultimate hope.

There is a man who discovers that his most acute concepts and most intellectually refined operations of the mind do not fit; that the unity of consciousness and that of which one is conscious in the destruction of all systems is now to be found only in pain; that he cannot resolve the immeasurable multitude of questions, and yet cannot keep to the clearly known content of individual experience and to the sciences.

There is one who suddenly notices how the tiny trickle of his life wanders through the wilderness of the banality of existence, apparently without aim and with the heartfelt fear of complete exhaustion. And yet he hopes, he knows not how, that this trickle will find the infinite expanse of the ocean, even though it may still be covered by the grey sands which seem to extend for ever before him.

One could go on like this for ever, perhaps even then without coming to that experience which for this or that man is the experience of the Spirit, freedom and grace in his life. For every man makes that experience in accordance with the particular historical and individual situation of his specific life. Every man! But he has so to speak to dig it out from under the rubbish of everyday experience, and must not run away from it where it begins to become legible, as though it were only an undermining and disturbance of self-evidence of his everyday life and his scientific assurance.

Let me repeat, though I must say it in almost the same words: where the one and entire hope is given beyond all individual hopes, which comprehends all impulses in silent promise,

—where a responsibility in freedom is still accepted and borne where it has no apparent offer of success and advantage,

—where a man experiences and accepts his ultimate freedom which no earthly compulsions can take away from him,

—where the leap into the darkness of death is accepted as the beginning of everlasting promise,

—where the sum of all accounts of life, which no one can calculate alone, is understood by an inconceivable Other as good, though it still cannot be "proven",

—where the fragmentary experience of love, beauty, and joy is experienced and accepted purely and simply as the promise of love, beauty, and joy, without their being understood in ultimate cynical scepticism as a cheap form of consolation for some final deception,

—where the bitter, deceptive and vanishing everyday world is withstood until the accepted end, and accepted out of a force whose ultimate source is still unknown to us but can be tapped by us,

—where one dares to pray into a silent darkness and knows that one is heard, although no answer seems to come back about which one might argue and rationalize,

—where one lets oneself go unconditionally and experiences this capitulation as true victory,

—where falling becomes true uprightness,

—where desperation is accepted and is still secretly accepted as trustworthy without cheap trust,

—where a man entrusts all this knowledge and all his questions to the silent and all-inclusive mystery which is loved more than all our individual knowledge which makes us such small people.

—where we rehearse our own deaths in everyday life, and try to live in such a way as we would like to die, peaceful and composed,

—where . . . (as I have said, we could go on and on):

—there is God and his liberating grace. There we find what

we Christians call the Holy Spirit of God. Then we experience something which is inescapable (even when suppressed) in life, and which is offered to our freedom with the question whether we want to accept it or whether we want to shut ourselves up in a hell of freedom by trying to barricade ourselves against it. There is the mysticism of everyday life, the discovery of God in all things; there is the sober intoxication of the Spirit, of which the Fathers and the liturgy speak which we cannot reject or despise, because it is real'.[32]

Nothing needs to be added to what Rahner says here.

The Salvation of Non-Christians

The question of the possibility of the salvation of non-Christians is closely connected with this statement about man's experience of grace, including the experience of those who do not believe or who reject faith. This is not quite the same theme as that of 'anonymous Christianity', which will be discussed fully in the following chapter, but it is closely related to it and I shall attempt to provide an answer to the problem on the basis of Rahner's teaching.

The teaching of the Catholic Church that there is no salvation outside the community of the Church is not only very old—it is also a defined and therefore infallible statement. During the pontificate of Eugenius IV, the Fathers of the Council of Florence (1438–1445) discussed a pronouncement made a thousand years previously by Fulgentius, the bishop of Ruspe, and concluded: 'that no one outside the Catholic Church, neither pagans, nor Jews, nor heretics, nor schismatics, can participate in eternal life, but will go into the eternal fire that has been prepared for the devil and his angels, unless they are brought into the flock of the Catholic Church before their death'.[33]

Such statements, which insist on faith in God's revelation

of himself in the Word and in baptism—even that of children—if grace and salvation are to be obtained, have often been made in the history of the Church and they are all based on the sentence: *Extra Ecclesiam nulla salus* ('Outside the Church there is no supernatural salvation'). To be quite fair, however, it should not be forgotten that this dogmatic pronouncement was made when the one Christian faith was universally accepted by all men in what was geographically a very small world. It was known that other people existed elsewhere, but these people were, as it were, 'curiosities', and did not present the Church with any real problem of missionary work. It was possible for the salvation of these people to be regarded as taking place in a miraculous way.

This conviction has changed, very slowly, over the centuries, until the present, when we accept, almost without question, that there are millions of people who have never even heard of Christian faith. We also know, on the basis of the pluralism of the modern era and the sociological pattern that prevails today, that there are countless people as well who do not believe as Christians either because they are not familiar with Christian faith or for other reasons, for example: because they are influenced by various other philosophies; because they do not regard it as worthwhile to examine the claims of Christianity; because the faith of Christians makes too little impression on them; because they have already rejected faith and so on. We can summarize this situation in all its complexity by saying that there are people in our immediate environment and in the greater world who are no better and no worse than ourselves, but who are not Christians for a multiplicity of reasons.

This fact has confronted Christians with the question of whether these innumerable people can be saved. Can the Christian continue to think, as a member of a small fraction of the human race, that only that fraction is able to be saved by God? Rahner has expressed the modern Christian viewpoint very well. Modern man, he believes, feels that he is solidly united with the whole of humanity. With his heightened sense of history, he feels, Rahner has pointed out, that his place is with his fellow men and he does not want a heaven from which they are excluded in advance.

Because faith presupposes that all men are included and no one is excluded, there is clearly a crisis in faith here and Rahner is undoubtedly the first theologian to have pointed the way to a solution of the problem. It is possible to find without difficulty texts in Rahner's writings that correspond closely to what was said at the Second Vatican Council about the possible salvation of non-Christians.[34] (The Council stressed that the possibility existed, but did not discuss in detail how that salvation might be achieved.) One aspect of the problem is clear, however, and that is that the solution is not made difficult simply and solely by the dogma that there is no salvation outside the Church. There is the additional fact that it is just not possible for a person to achieve supernatural salvation simply and solely by means of his own good will, as so many seem to think now. As Rahner himself has said, the doctrine of the anonymous Christian does not imply that anyone, simply because he does not go against his own moral conscience, can be justified and definitively saved without faith in a strictly theological sense. It is clearly assumed, both in Pius XII's document of 1949 against the rigorism of Leonard Feeney, and in the teaching of the Second Vatican Council, that a *fides supernaturalis* is required even in the case of a justified pagan, in other words, a supernatural faith that can only be made possible by God and is, in the last resort, God himself. Why, Rahner asks in the same context, are supernatural faith, hope, and love required for the supernatural salvation of every person?

To answer this question, we must first point out that man's supernatural salvation in this world and especially in the

next is not an additional reward for virtue practised on earth
that is dependent on God's good will. Salvation is rather a
making eternal of what has already taken place here on
earth. This implies that it is not possible for salvation to be
achieved unless man's life has become assimilated to God's
through the supernatural virtues of faith, hope, and love.
Connected with this is the fact that Christianity is not like
Buddhism or Islam, for example, in which a prophet, a
Buddha or a Mohammed died and left a religion behind
that was able to continue after the death of its founder (and
thus, strictly speaking, without that founder). In the Christian view, man's salvation is inseparably linked with the
person of Jesus of Nazareth, to such an extent that the
necessary pre-condition for the salvation of man is to be
accepted into the body of Christ (and in his death and
resurrection). Man's salvation is not based on truths communicated by God (however necessary dogmatic formulae may
be). Man is sanctified and saved because, in Christ, he shares
in God's life. What we have, then, is a supernatural mode of
being which cannot be attributed to man as it were arbitrarily or posthumously even by God. This is, according to
Rahner, how the statement *Extra Ecclesiam nulla salus* should
be understood and the Catholic Church continues to claim
that it is true in this sense. This leads us to the next question,
which is, how is it possible for the pagan or the non-
Christian to have this faith? Two factors have to be borne in
mind in any attempt to answer this question, and Rahner has
considered both of them. The first is the universal will of
God to save all men. The second is the relationship between
nature and supernature.

The doctrine of God's universal will to save is as old as the
Church itself. It is God's will that all men without exception
should be saved, that Christ's work of redemption should
not be restricted to one particular group of people, and that
the Church should have the task of proclaiming and

bringing salvation to all peoples, races, and nations. There is such clear evidence of this in Scripture and the documents of the Church's teaching office that I have no need to discuss it further here. It is, however, important to add that, in the past, this universal will of God to save all men was, by and large, restricted in practice to those who accepted the explicit teaching of the Church and were baptized in the Church. It is difficult now to see how God's universal will to save can be interpreted as an authentic will to save all men if it is to be restricted in this way. One has only to think of those many people whom the Gospel simply did not reach. It is easy to devalue the universal will of God to save all men to the level of mere good will, which is in itself limited and even self-contradictory. If this tendency is to be avoided, God's saving will has to be taken seriously as applying to all men. God's will in this as in every other case is not simply a well meant declaration of intention hidden in the depths of God's heart. On the contrary, it is a reality in man and in every man. What God wants is real. If God wants all men to be saved, that is a fact that changes man and creates a reality. What, then, is the concrete manifestation of this will to save? I must consider this now in the context of Rahner's theology.

When I was discussing man's transcendental experiences, I considered the important part played by the inner dynamism of man's spirituality. Rahner takes this inner dynamism as his point of departure here and calls it a supernatural existential factor in man. In other words, this dynamic element in man's transcendental experiences is never purely natural. It is always supernatural, with the result that even the non-Christian performs supernatural actions, that is, actions which contain within themselves a reference to his supernatural salvation in God.

Rahner explains this phenomenon in the following way. We ought not to think of the supernatural grace of faith and justification offered by God to men as an intermittent intervention by God in a world that is in itself profane. In the light of God's universal will to save, it should be understood as an existential element of the spiritual creature and the world as such, which sums up this secular history in the direction of the immediacy of God. The existential factor is always given as an offer of grace. God's universal will to save, which is always made objective in God's communication of himself in grace given in the mode of an offer and a making possible of saving action, is, although it is supernatural, the innermost entelechy[35] and dynamism of the world as the history of the spiritual creature. As a dynamism, it does not have to be known in reflection or objectively, but it is always present.

This grace, Rahner says, forms a permanent part of man's being as a dynamism and a final summation of human history and is known as a conscious factor, but not necessarily as objective knowledge, in the *a priori* formal objects,[36] and in the spheres of spiritually intentional capacities for knowledge and freedom. Whether man knows this reflectively or not, and whether he is able to reflect about it and apply it to himself or not, he nonetheless finishes by the grace that is offered to him as his freedom in the mode of a formal object and a spiritual *a priori* sphere in the direction of the immediacy of God. He leads his spiritual life in knowledge and freedom in such a way that God is in himself the ultimate direction of his history of knowledge and freedom, not as the God of metaphysical knowledge or the God of infinite distance, but as the God who, in himself and in his own reality and glory, is the ultimate aim, in other words, as the God of eternal life.

Rahner therefore concludes that there is a real and supernatural possibility of salvation for non-Christians only if God's universal will to save is an effective will, and as such capable of creating a real possibility of salvation in each man.

The Possibility of Faith in Revelation

In addition to man's experience of grace and the need to concede that there is a real possibility of salvation for non-Christians, there is another question that has to be considered before I go on to discuss whether we are justified in assuming that the supernatural existential element exists in all men and before we deal with the relationship between nature and grace. That is the question of the possibility of a supernatural knowledge of revelation. It can be expressed in the following way: For Christian faith, revelation is a supernatural revelation of God, which is free on God's part (and therefore not owed to man) and which, on man's part, poses the question as to how he is able to know such a supernatural revelation of God as a supernatural revelation so that God's word does not simply disappear, but can be known as his definitive word and not regarded merely as one of many—more or less—prophetic words uttered in the course of human history.

However God's revelation may be represented, it can certainly only take place in a spatio-temporal, categorial mediation, in other words, in history, in the word and in the self-exposition of a man. There is, therefore, always the danger that it will be regarded as no more than simply a human word in the history of mankind. The traditional Catholic answer to this question is to be found in the so-called doctrine of the *analysis fidei,* in which it has to be demonstrated that man is able to find a direct way to God mediated in signs and that he must also be empowered, in the act of faith, by the supernatural grace of God to believe supernaturally. Despite individual controversies, it has always been obvious to Catholic theologians that, subject to these conditions, man has always needed a supernatural light of faith; that is, he has always had to be raised up supernaturally by grace before being able to give his consent to faith. As Rahner himself has pointed out, God's disclosure of himself in the human word of revelation would cease to exist if it were not closely linked to the inner light of grace and strictly supernatural faith. If God—insofar as he is the one who has not been made known by his creation which is different from him—were to speak about himself in the human word without the listening subject being raised up supernaturally, his speaking in this way would be subject to the subjective *a priori* of the finite spirit alone. It would also, if it did not simply cease to exist, be reduced to an aspect of self-understanding of pure nature and therefore cease to be a real self-disclosure on the part of God.

As I have said, this has always been known in the Catholic theology of faith. Until Rahner took the question up, however, insufficient attention had been devoted to this gift of grace to man as a necessary pre-condition of faith. It was regarded as necessary if the supernatural quality of faith was to be guaranteed, but it was also thought to be present only when man was directly confronted with the decision to believe. If we disregard the need to speak about grace as a later addition to the theological definition of faith, Rahner claims, the character of faith as hearing is interpreted *a posteriori* and empirically on the basis of certain dogmatic statements which reveal that what is addressed by this word of faith as hearing seems almost to be a formal ability to understand some true statement that is comprehended insofar as it is made familiar to the hearer in a correct, legitimate and suitable way. Hardly any thought has been given by Catholic theologians, Rahner once said, to the *a priori* capacity to believe. But how is it possible for God's personal revelation of himself not to take place at the finite level of the finite creature, Rahner has asked. It is only possible if there is an ontological deification of man which is already present in freedom, even though it is not accepted by that freedom in faith. It is possible, in other words, if the fundamental datum of man's ultimate sphere of knowledge and freedom within which he expresses his existence is transcendentally deified. Faith can, in the sense of an analogous experience, be brought about by a lasting gift of grace by God to man, that is, by means of this supernatural existential factor (which at the same time also contains the transcendental aspect of God's revelation of himself). The spatio-temporal and historical revelation of God's word comes to man who is also, on the basis of his supernatural existential element, always *a priori*—and transcendentally— oriented towards this word of God in history and is, as it were, always waiting for this word of revelation as a promise of salvation.

How, then, can the supernatural revelation of God that is mediated categorially be known as God's revelation? Rahner is not alone in the answer that he gives to this question. It is only possible, he says, if the external revela- tion of God corresponds to an inner aspect of transcenden- tal, supernatural experience in man, with the result that knowledge of revelation is at the same time an analogous experience of the external and the inner word of God made possible by grace, so that the word of God can be accepted as such in faith within the context of its categorial appearance.

This inner grace is the supernatural existential aspect in man which Rahner, as we have seen, regards as permanently present in man and not simply as something that immediate- ly precedes the act of faith. In the light of this conviction, he is therefore able to claim that, if—in the event of revelation and faith—God himself is, in his communication of himself, what is believed and the *a priori* principle of faith, then the logic of faith is not a logic acquired categorially from

outside, but, like the original natural logic, the inner
ontological structure of the act of faith itself. If, Rahner goes
on, the external message of faith mediates not the *a posteriori*
reason for faith, but the *a priori* structure of immediacy with
itself, then the problem is without an object. The external
revelation of God, in which he communicates himself to
man, can therefore be known as a revelation of God. This
automatically gives it an existential significance; this becomes even clearer in the light of the relationship between
nature and grace.

The Relationship between Nature and Grace

I have already said that the original impetus that led Rahner
to introduce the idea of the supernatural existential element
in all men was provided by the doctrine of grace: the
teaching that has played such an important part in relatively
recent Catholic theology and that has, moreover, had
negative effects on faith. To reduce this matter to a single
and brief common denominator, God's grace must inevitably be seen as something that is added to human nature,
which is as it is even without grace. This is so in spite of the
fact that God is not in any way indebted to man for grace
and that the effect of grace is to liberate man. It is also so,
however much emphasis is placed on the necessity of grace
for salvation and on its supernatural character.

Rahner has pointed out that the relationship between
nature and grace has been presented in such a way that the
two elements are seen as on two carefully distinguished
levels, one superimposed on the other and that the orientation of nature towards grace is viewed in a negative way. It is
true, he agrees, that grace is a unique way of perfecting
nature and that God, as the one who is Lord over man's
nature, can require man to be subject to his will as it exists, to
recognize it as giving life and as a supernatural aim and to

be open to receive grace. In itself, however, nature has only the *potentia oboedientialis* and this has been seen in a very negative light, as an element that does not contradict the raising up of nature. It is not possible, Rahner has correctly concluded, to claim that this average presentation of the case is entirely free from what has been called 'extrinsecism'. Attention has rightly been drawn to the fact that God's grace, when presented in this way, is seen as a superstructure added to the soul or even as an ornament and not as the real centre of man's existence. Since God and his grace are seen as added to man's being, even though this addition may be the ultimate perfection of human nature, God cannot therefore be regarded as the innermost aim and ultimate longing of man.

The usual point of departure in the traditional theology of grace is our understanding of human nature and of natural man. According to this concept man, who does not know the categorial revelation of God's word or else is guilty in his refusal to believe in that revelation, is always natural man. Man is natural in this way either because he is in sin or because he simply cannot reach faith because of a lack of knowledge of God's revelation in Jesus Christ. The explicit connection made between salvation and the possibility of salvation on the one hand, and knowledge of and faith in the revelation of God's word on the other, closed the door to the possibility of salvation for a non-Christian. The man who rejected faith seemed also to refer to the purely natural state and thus to incur serious guilt, but only because God, as it were, decrees acceptance of his revelation from outside. Is, then, man's destiny in God not taken seriously enough? Rahner has suggested that, however much supernatural grace may transcend the nature of the spiritual being, man, this does not mean that God's communication of himself can be a matter of indifference to the creature. The extrinsecism of the traditional theology of grace is therefore based on the fact that, on the one hand, God's gift of supernatural grace to man is linked to the Christian message and the hearing of the Gospel, because it is only in this way that man can come to faith (at least this is how it seemed to those who propounded this traditional theology, and in principle they were not wrong); and, on the other hand, that sanctifying grace was regarded by these theologians as a perfection that was added to man, that is to say, as an 'accident'. The result was that they were unable to demonstrate clearly how this grace could at the same time fulfil man's innermost dynamism and impel him towards the end to which he was, in his innermost being, oriented.

In the nineteen-forties, various French members of the movement known as the *Nouvelle théologie*[37] set themselves the task of rethinking this problem of the relationship between nature and grace and postulated a *desiderium naturale visionis beatificae,* which was basically a theological view that had been freely expressed by Thomas Aquinas. Pius XII intervened in 1943 with his encyclical *Mystici Corporis* and insisted that God's freedom and the gratuitous character of supernatural grace were not sufficiently guaranteed if man as it were of his own accord, that is, as a pure creature and in his purely natural state, were thought to have a right to the beatific vision that was only possible through the free and supernatural grace of God.

God's grace is gratuitous for two reasons. As Rahner has pointed out, God's free communication of himself is gratuitous grace and an unexpected initiative taken by his free, divine love both insofar as we are finite creatures and insofar as we are sinners. These two reasons must, Rahner believes, be clearly distinguished, although they form a unity in the one man. For both reasons God's grace is never something that can be merited.

Rahner knows the problem very well and has found a solution so simple and penetrating that it is hardly disputed today. In order to overcome the extrinsecism of grace, he insists on the possibility of a pure human nature that has not been finalized supernaturally and in this way ensures that God's grace is free and gratuitous. At the same time, however, he maintains that this possibility has never been a reality. In concrete terms this means that man, in his factual existence, is not pure nature and does not experience himself as such. In the sense of a supernatural existential factor, grace is always present for every man as *a priori,* transcendental consciousness and as an offer made by God that precedes every act and decision made by man and all his knowledge. As an offer made by God and as God's concrete will to save all men, this supernatural existential element is a reality in man, with the result that every man is dynamically finalized in the direction of God's grace, which is God himself, and this finalization takes place in the innermost depths of being. The condition of man's possibility, we are bound to say, is not simply a natural transcendence. It is also a supernatural finalization. Man is always *a priori,* that is, before he performs his acts of knowledge and freedom, subject to God's call and effective saving will. Man's factual nature, Rahner has pointed out more than once, is never 'pure' nature, but nature situated in a supernatural dispensation from which man—even unbelieving and sinful man—cannot escape the nature that is always being transformed (not, it should be noted, necessarily justified) by the supernatural saving grace offered by God.

The supernatural existential factor is, Rahner has pointed out again and again, an offer made to man, not a justification of man and God's will to save man is therefore a reality that determines man's life and being, even if he rejects God in sin. It is not possible to dispense with the concept of pure human nature if the idea of grace as gratuitous for two reasons is to be safeguarded. This pure nature is, however, only a contrasting concept and not a reality in man, within which it is no longer possible to distinguish between what man is in the light of pure nature, and what he is *de facto*, and therefore what he experiences in his transcendental experiences as the supernatural raising up of his existence: in other words, as the supernatural existential element in his life.

We cannot say, then, what man—or the human spirit—would be without God's grace, because we have never experienced ourselves without that grace, and because we are also determined by that grace even when we reject it in sin or guilt. What I have said so far implies that Rahner believes that the supernatural call made to man by God's grace is given not simply ontically, but also ontologically. In other words, it is present not only in the order of man's being, but also in some form in man's consciousness, which it determines in some way. This grace, he has said, transforms our conscious life, not only our being, but also our existence.

Rahner said this about nature and grace in an interview a few years ago: 'As soon as what is called grace is seen to be a state in which man's self-expression and activity are borne up by God's communication of himself and as soon as grace is accepted as a constitutive, transcendental structure in man, a change takes place in the relationship between nature and grace. That relationship—between creation and grace or between our natural knowledge of God and the theology of revelation—can no longer be understood as something that is added or exists at different levels, in other words, in the way in which it was understood in recent centuries from the late scholastic period onwards. There is no single human action in which God does not communicate himself to us, in which, in other words, his grace is not, either reflectively or unreflectively, at work and aspects of revelation are involved. It is simply not possible for man, who has grace as an existential aspect of his existence that cannot be avoided, to make a clear distinction, within what he calls to mind verbally and in reflection concerning himself and his world, between what has to be attributed to revelation and what is simply due to a natural knowledge of God, in other words, what is natural freedom and what is freedom as the result of grace. Distinctions such as those made between nature and grace, revelation and natural metaphysics and the natural law and the supernatural moral law are justified from the methodological point of view, because grace is gratuitous, but they are secondary and additional distinctions'.

Rahner describes what is ontically present in man and what takes place in his being as God's communication of himself. (The relationship between created and uncreated grace can not be applied here, since this would introduce us to the sphere of theology of grace.) For Rahner, however, grace is first and foremost a self-communication by God in his Trinitarian reality. Since everything that is created can, at least in theory, always be natural, Rahner is only able to regard supernatural grace as God's communcation of himself to man. This is why he is not able to deny or obscure the fact that created grace is an effect of uncreated grace, even though grace is first and foremost uncreated grace, that is, God's sharing of himself with and communication of himself to man, a concept which is, according to Vorgrimler, possibly the most important in his whole theology.

Rahner himself maintains that this divine self-communication has deifying effects in the finite being in whom the self-communication takes place, effects which, as definitions of a finite subject, must themselves be regarded as finite and created. If this were not the case, man would participate in God and not simply in his life. The most distinctive aspect of God's communication of himself, however, is that it points to a relationship between God and the finite being, who can and must be understood in analogy to a causality, in which the cause becomes the inner constitutive

principle of what is itself caused. Rahner does not accept the
existence of a created grace that is different from God,
because everything that is created by God is different from
him and is, according to its essential being, a creature and
not divine in its mode of being. It is obvious that God's
communication of himself to man has consequences in man
which are 'created', but it does not cease to be God's
self-communication, since what God brings about by this
self-communication he brings about by means of a 'formal
causality' or a 'quasi-formal causality', as Rahner has called
it.[38] By this, he means that this self-communication should
not be thought of as an efficient or effective causality, but
that something becomes the constitutive principle of something else without ceasing to be what it is. This is ultimately
the absolute prerogative of God himself, since, as Rahner
has pointed out, only the absolute being of God is able to set
aside from itself what is different from God without
becoming subject to the difference from him and to communicate itself as itself without losing itself in that communication.

To summarize what is contained in this chapter, we may
say that the supernatural existential element in man is a
concept that has been introduced into Catholic theology by
Rahner to express the fact that every man—even the man
who does not know or rejects God's categorial revelation of
himself in Jesus Christ—is never simply 'natural' man, but is
always subject to the active and effective saving will of God.
This will to save is a reality which determines *a priori* man's
fundamental situation, finalizes the dynamism of his spirituality towards his supernatural end in God and therefore
constitutes the innermost element of his being. Although
this supernatural gift of grace to man (which is present, for
example, in his transcendental experience) is always consciously given to all men (although they do not always know
it), it is always a gratuitous gift to man as a creature and a

sinner, in other words, all men are permanently subject to God's offer of grace that is really effective in them and this situation is inevitable and lasting.

God's will to save and redeem all men in Jesus Christ is a reality in man which precedes all personal knowledge and every act of freedom. The supernatural existential element, which in this case is an experience of grace, enables man to acquire a supernatural formal object, that is, to experience himself and to see his world in the light of God's supernatural grace. All the same, this supernatural existential factor is no more than an offer of salvation. In the full sense of the word, grace itself is man's consent, freely accepted and made possible by God's grace, to this offer of grace. No man is able, even if he rejects the offer of grace or is in sin, to escape from this supernatural existential dispensation, the ontic aspect of which appearing ontologically: in other words, the aspect of the supernatural existential factor in man that is in accordance with his being appears in accordance with his consciousness—with the result that man, whether he knows or recognizes it or not, both possesses and acknowledges the supernatural existential factor as an inner aspect of his own subjectivity (and does this transcendentally).

This supernatural existential factor is, as we have already seen in this chapter, of great importance in Rahner's doctrine of faith, in his teaching about the universal will of God to save all men and in his outline of the relationship between nature and grace. As we shall also see in the following chapter, it plays an important part in his concept of the universal revelation of God, his evaluation of the non-Christian religions and his theory of anonymous Christianity and, finally, his Christology.

·5·

Anonymous Christianity and God's Universal Revelation

Rahner's teaching about the supernatural existential factor and God's offer of supernatural grace forms the very heart of his theology, but, in demonstrating the need for this supernatural existential element at the centre of man's existence and discussing its ramifications, I have dealt only with part of Rahner's whole theological work. I have said nothing, for example, about his reflections on the Church or its sacraments and the question of office in the Church, his examination of the doctrine of indulgences, his consideration of the Trinity or his teaching about human sin, including original sin, and the relationship between the love of God and one's neighbour, which is important in this context. Nothing has been said either about death, dying, Mariology, the future of theology or the training of theologians.

Rahner has spoken and written about all these questions and many others, but however important and pioneering they may be for Catholic theology, they cannot be considered here. What cannot be avoided, if we are to understand Rahner and his work at all, is a consideration of the concept of the supernatural existential element in man that is at the centre of his theological teaching and the consequences that result from this. These consequences are unambiguous evidence of the originality of Rahner's thought and would have been unthinkable twenty or thirty years ago. He himself has often expressed surprise that his theology has not been more violently attacked by the neo-scholastic theologians of the Church, who have accepted it relatively quietly, although it cannot be easily reconciled with their teaching, which is more obviously in accordance with the Catholic tradition of the past hundred years or so.

I think that there are two main reasons for this.[39] In the first place, there are fewer and fewer neo-scholastic theologians now and their places have been taken increasingly by theologians who accept Rahner's ideas as a matter of course. In the second place, Rahner's theology is, in most cases, far more closely attuned to the present-day crisis in faith. His life has been spent in a constant search for a theological answer to the problems of contemporary man in his faith and doubt, with the result that a return to traditional neo-scholasticism and a possible rejection of Rahner's theology is very unlikely. These are two reasons why his work has been attacked so little—there may be other or better reasons, but I do not know any.

In the interview in which he spoke of the supernatural existential element in man as his fundamental theological conviction, he went on to say that one of the most important consequences of that concept was what he called 'anonymous Christianity' and insisted: 'I know of no religion of any kind in which the grace of God is not present, however suppressed or depraved it may be in its expression. Another consequence is what I have called the transcendental aspect of historical revelation'.

I have already considered the possibility of salvation for non-Christians in the previous chapter. I stressed, I think sufficiently, that this was a possibility—even the Christian has no complete certainty with regard to his own salvation.[40] There is, however, a possibility that non-Christians will be saved. Unlike the traditional neo-scholastic theologians of the Church, who believed that no one could be an atheist for a long period without incurring guilt, the Fathers of the Second Vatican Council were of the opinion that it was possible for an atheist of very long standing to have an attitude of faith, hope, and love, an attitude which could, Rahner is convinced, bring about salvation. He has said in this context that a man may have almost any attitude, but he cannot be denied a possibility of salvation. It is only if we concede that salvation is possible that we can be said to be taking quite seriously the biblical statement that we should not judge others.

What does this mean in concrete terms? It means that we cannot state whether, when or under what conditions the non-Christian's salvation will be achieved and that we cannot judge who is closer to salvation—a militant atheist, an agnostic who is at a distance from the Church, a pious pagan, or even a believing Christian. This is so even if there may be objective criteria for the truth of a religion. There are two important questions that have to be asked in this chapter and I shall attempt to provide an answer for them. The first is: What does Rahner mean by 'anonymous Christians'? The second is: How should the non-Christian religions—or philosophies—be evaluated in the light of Christian faith, if a transcendental aspect of supernatural revelation is present in them?

Is the Concept of Anonymous Christians Offensive?

Rahner calls those who achieve salvation without any knowledge of the historical, categorial revelation of God's word 'anonymous Christians' and speaks in this context of 'anonymous Christianity'. He has tried in numerous articles to define what he means by this term, since it can be and has been misunderstood. Misunderstanding arises less in connection with the content of the phrase, since the possibility of the salvation of non-Christians can no longer be seriously disputed since the Second Vatican Council, than on the basis of the expression itself. Is it possible, for example, that Rahner may have chosen the wrong name for the right theme? Or: What does he mean by explicit Christianity if explicitly Christian faith is not required, according to him, it would seem, for salvation? I must consider these and similar objections to his theory of anonymous Christianity here.

The objections to Rahner's anonymous Christianity can, I think, be reduced to three headings. The first is that the name does not really suit the matter covered. The second is that the doctrine of anonymous Christianity is an offensive taking over of non-Christians. The third is that it is a relativization of Christianity.

In the case of the first objection, Rahner himself has left us in no doubt that he does not insist on the name or the terminology he uses. He has confessed that the terminology does not really matter very much. Anyone who admits the existence of what is indicated by these particular words, he has said, and has another, perhaps better word which will express the same matter in a clearer way can easily dispense with his terminology. He has admitted that he has to continue to use the words 'anonymous Christian' until someone suggests a better phrase and this clearly indicates that the battle is not really about words, but about the matter itself.

On the one hand, it is important not to overlook the word 'Christianity'. If the intention is not to by-pass the real theological task and leave aside any consideration of how it may be possible for non-Christians to achieve salvation, this vital aspect of Christianity cannot simply be excluded from the possibility of salvation. It can only be excluded if the claim is made that there are other ways to salvation apart from that brought about by Christ, which is unthinkable for the Christian. On the other hand, the fact that such Christianity is not explicit emerges from the matter itself.

In this context, it is worth looking at some of the polemical arguments that have been used against Rahner's doctrine. I do not find them convincing. Jüngel, for example, has said that Christianity is, in its very essence, not only not anonymous, but also quite hostile to anonymity. Christian faith is not only known by the name of the one to whom it owes its existence and to whom it refers, but also requires to be known by that name and associated with it.[41] Jüngel may well be right in this and I would not wish to dispute it, but neither he nor any of the other opponents of Rahner's terminology have suggested any alternative terminology that can be used equally well to express what is meant, without introducing a severe limitation upon that content.

Hans Küng, for example, has spoken of a 'more radical humanity'[42] and Jüngel has used the phrase 'a more human humanity'[43] as possibly applying to the explicit Christian. This implies, however, that, whether it is intentional or not, a defective form of human existence is attributed to the non-Christian. It is, of course, true that the theological doctrine of anonymous Christianity contains a suggestion that the humanity of the non-Christian is in some way defective; otherwise it would be possible and indeed necessary to save oneself the effort of missionary work and evangelization. Rahner, however, recognizes that this deficiency is a deficiency of the explicit, reflective consciousness which has an effect on practical life. He insists, on the other hand, that the humanity of the non-Christian exists at the same supernatural, radical, and human level as that of the explicit Christian. The question that confronts him is, after all: If I recognize that it is possible for all men to be saved and do not believe that salvation is never achieved outside explicit Christianity and if I know, as a Christian, that all supernatural salvation is related to Jesus Christ and that there is no salvation outside Christ, what am I to call those who achieve that salvation? Should I suppress the fact that this salvation must be Christian? Should I do this, even though there is a danger that Christianity would at first sight thereby appear to be given a relative value? Let someone suggest a better term . . . !

The second objection, namely that Rahner's doctrine of anonymous Christianity may be an offensive taking over of non-Christians, has been raised more and more frequently in recent years. Jüngel formulated it as a question: 'Does this teaching not amount to an injury to the non-Christian's self-respect if he finds himself referred to as an anonymous Christian in his absence or even addressed as such. Used in this way, the term "anonymous Christian" can easily go beyond its original intention and become offensive'.[44]

In arguing in this way, Jüngel and others have, I believe, failed to see that it is not a question, in this doctrine of anonymous Christianity, of imposing anything on non-Christians that they would themselves not want to be or even of trying to increase the rapidly diminishing number of Christians by letting others in through the back door. The question of anonymous Christianity is simply and solely a question that applies within the Christian framework itself. It is *my* question, not that of non-Christians. As a believing Christian, I am bound to ask myself about the situation with regard to the salvation of those whom I see around me and who are no worse or more stupid or more malicious than I am, but who are not Christians and who do not want to be Christians.

Schlette is correct in his judgment of Rahner's thesis of the anonymous Christian. He has pointed out that Rahner sees this thesis 'from the methodical point of view as dogmatic and theological. In other words, it can only be accepted on the basis of the explicit faith of the (Protestant or Catholic) Church and non-Christians are not even expected to understand or accept this thesis'.[45] The theology of the anonymous Christian should therefore be seen as an answer which a Christian, and only a Christian, is able and indeed obliged to give to the question that he asks about the possibility of the salvation of those who are not Christian.

Rahner's theologoumenon of the anonymous Christian was never intended to be an apologetical instrument, nor can it be used as such. I do not want to convince the non-Christian that he is not what he explicitly confesses himself to be. I do not have to tell him that he is not what he is or what he wants to be. I do, however, as a believing Christian, have to ask myself whether I am one of the few who has been 'chosen' or whether what I believe and hope is not also there for others. It is surely not offensive to the non-Christian to attribute positively to him the good that I believe I have myself, not in a direct encounter with him, but in my own conscience. Would I feel offended or think that I was being taken over if a Marxist or an atheist were to say that he found what is good and valuable in his own attitude in me? Finally, do I not really know at least something that I cannot, without being dishonest in my faith, simply deny to the non-Christian? In a word, it is, in my opinion, difficult to understand and very regrettable that the theology of anonymous Christianity should be attacked and reduced to this low and almost unworthy level. The level of argument should surely be much higher!

A Relativization of Christian Faith?

The third objection that is often raised to Rahner's argument is that Christianity may be given a relative value by it and that it may be made so unimportant that it will no longer be necessary to preach, convert, missionize, or evangelize. Hans Urs von Balthasar, for example, has rejected Rahner's theologoumenon of anonymous Christianity because 'it implies a relativization of the objective revelation of God in the biblical event and a sanctioning of the objective religious ways of other religions as ordinary and extraordinary ways of salvation'.[46] It is difficult to see how Balthasar can reconcile this statement with those made at Vatican II, but that is his affair. What I cannot understand is how it is possible to maintain that non-Christians have a possibility of salvation on the one hand and, on the other, not to recognize an 'extraordinary' way of salvation in the other religions.

The criticisms made by Balthasar and others, however, undoubtedly have a much more serious purpose. These critics recognize that to attribute to those who are not explicitly Christian the possibility of reaching the aim of human life, culminating in the vision of God, is to make a deep, perhaps fatal incision into the whole Christian tradition and view of faith. The question as to whether Christian faith is not necessary for salvation and whether the specific quality of Christian faith may be levelled down is one that arises with some urgency. This question cannot be answered easily or at once, because it contains three aspects which have to be examined separately.

The first of these aspects is the old question: *Cur Deus homo?* This can be expressed in concrete as: If God had not been able to bring about man's salvation, he would not have become man. Assuming that there is what Rahner calls a supernatural existential factor, and that this extends to man's salvation, why did God become man? Anyone asking this particular question in this way is obviously questioning the connection between man's salvation and the incarnation, cross, and resurrection of Christ and, what is more, he is asking about it in the sense that the incarnation of God is simply a pre-condition for man's salvation as such, in other words, that there would not have been an incarnation of God if there had been no supernatural salvation for man.

This questioning is quite legitimate, but I shall try to answer it in a more suitable context, at the end of the next chapter.[47]

The second question, however, is quite different. It is this. I may recognize that there would have been no salvation for man if the Logos had not become man, but I may still ask, particularly within the context of anonymous Christianity and the problems that this thesis raises, what change is made in my situation of salvation by my explicit knowledge, as a Christian, of Jesus' work of redemption in word and deed. Why and in what way am I better off if I profess myself explicitly to be a Christian?

The third question that forms part of the original question is how the salvation of non-Christians can be Christian, even though this may be an anonymous, unknown, and non-explicit Christianity, if nothing is known about Jesus Christ. This third question can be differently expressed: What is it that binds all men to Jesus Christ so that even the non-Christian achieves a really Christian salvation and receives the grace of God? How can the incarnation, the cross, and the resurrection of the Lord be made to relate in a real sense to the salvation of non-Christians if we presuppose that salvation only exists and can only exist in Jesus Christ?

Let me now consider the last two questions by presupposing that there could be no salvation without the incarnation of God in Jesus of Nazareth, and ask what advantage explicit knowledge of God's revelation in Jesus Christ and an explicitly Christian faith has over anonymous Christianity or, to express this in a different way, why explicit faith in Jesus Christ is required by God. One thing ought to be clear even now. The 'plus' of explicit faith does not consist in the fact that only the Christian can achieve salvation. There is also a possibility of salvation outside Christian faith and outside the Church, even though this salvation will always of necessity be related to Christ and, in him, to the Church.

Why, then, does there have to be explicit Christianity?

One reason Rahner has suggested is that the believing Christian has a greater chance of salvation than the non-Christian. If a man knows more reflectively who he is, Rahner has said, and how he can express himself in freedom, there is a greater chance that he will be radically successful in this self-expression and perfection than if he expresses his humanity in a dull and unreflecting way. This is why the man who has previously been an anonymous Christian and has been brought to himself in reflection by missionary activity becomes, on the one hand, much more radically responsible and is, on the other, given a much greater chance to express this inner Christianity that has been given to him by grace in radical freedom and complete fulness as explicit Christianity.

Although this argument is convincing, I have the impression that Rahner does not insist on it strongly, since it may also give the appearance that, within the framework of explicit Christianity outlined in this way, the non-Christian is not necessarily denied a possibility of salvation, but that it is much more difficult for him than for the explicit Christian to achieve it. If, however, this argument is accepted within the framework of Rahner's total conception of anonymous Christianity, his real position at once becomes quite clear. The explicit knowledge of God's revelation of himself in Jesus Christ which the explicitly believing Christian, unlike the anonymous Christian, possesses is not simply a knowledge which may or may not be present and which has no influence on the life of the one who has it. On the contrary, this knowledge of faith is an existential knowledge which has a direct influence on life. Heinrich Ott has said in this context that the aspect of consciousness in Christian knowledge is not only a 'plus' in knowledge, but also a 'plus' in being, and results in a commitment of life in the light of faith.[48]

The real argument, on the basis of which Rahner inter-
prets a 'plus' in knowledge as a 'plus' in being, must
therefore be developed from the existential aspect of man's
knowledge of faith, and to understand this correctly we
must grasp what is meant by transcendental necessity in a
person's life and at the same time place oneself in the
position of an anonymous Christian. What does this mean?
On the one hand, on the basis of his supernatural finalization, man wants to know something about this inexpressible
mystery which is the direction and aim of his life. This
knowledge cannot simply be known in an obscure and dull
way. It does not always want to be simply nameless and
uncertain. A non-Christian, however, does not know, with
explicit knowledge, the closeness of God, his grace as a
communication of himself or his love and redemption. He is
therefore always in doubt, because he does not know
whether what he hopes and longs for in his innermost being
is a reality or will ever be a reality. Because he is a child of
our time, he is bound to relativize all religion and all
philosophy or else subscribe to the utopia of a salvation
that can be brought about within this world, knowing that
this secular salvation is always in the future, at least for
himself and probably—to express it very cautiously—for
all men.

On the other hand, however, to ask this question about
the necessity of explicit Christianity is inevitably to ask why
Jesus himself was a missionary: that is, why he proclaimed
salvation and claimed to have been sent by God, since it is
possible to think—even though the thought may be unreal,
because it has been superseded by history—that Christ
might have been able to carry out his task of redemption in
silence. It is, after all, conceivable that we might have been
redeemed by him without his making himself known as the
redeemer.

If we pursue this idea to its logical conclusion, we are bound to say that we would all be, in that situation at least, anonymous Christians today. But what would we be in that case? Would we not wish that God would redeem us from the anonymity of our salvation by his word? Would we not be in the position of those who have to hope without being able to give a concrete reason for or a name to that hope, and who are incapable of pointing to a moment in the history of the world where what, in spite of all man's expectations, transcends that expectation has been in fact fulfilled? In addition, would we not have to fear that all our faith, hope and love might be no more than a desire unconfirmed by God or a mere illusion which can be explained with transcendental necessity, although we can never know whether there will ever be fulfilment or whether it will ever be a reality?

The so-called Christian who regards faith simply as the sum total of additional duties and obligations, as a burden that is not imposed on a non-Christian, is beyond help in this matter. Such a person is bound to wish that he were himself an anonymous Christian so that he could achieve salvation as such. The situation is quite different in the case of a Christian who has found in faith what he has always looked for as a man, who knows that the nameless mystery has a name and that he can call him 'Father'. For him, God is not the eternal distance, but the forgiving and loving nearness, redeeming him from the torment of sceptical not knowing because he knows that, at a particular point in the history of the world, his future became a reality and that this future will be good. He knows that his salvation cannot cease to be, because the God who became man will never cease to be one of us. He knows too that he is redeemed from the idols of this world. He can encounter the world with inner peace and serenity in the knowledge that this world is not the only reality. He is also bound to commit himself to this world in an active expression of faith, hope, and love because he can only in this way achieve his salvation and he can only achieve it in freedom in this world.

In view of this, is it possible to ask seriously what the Christian has in his explicit faith if he were able to achieve salvation in a different way? It certainly happens that this question arises from time to time with some urgency and our only response can be simply to reflect again about the heart of the Gospel in order to experience the advantage that we as Christians have over anonymous Christians. In Jesus of Nazareth, I see that confirmed and know what I have always wished and hoped for in my innermost being. In addition to this, I am also able to regard the longing of the non-Christian as something that is different from that of the Christian. It is a longing that cannot be made explicit as such, so that Jesus Christ cannot simply be the fulfilment of what he wants to be. As a Christian, on the contrary, I know that I can never achieve this myself and alone and that I am told in the Gospel what I cannot tell myself, but what I hope for as the fulfilment of my life that is still to come.

This emerges in an even clearer light as soon as we turn our attention to another, related question. If the term 'anonymous Christianity' has any meaning at all, this is to be found in the fact that the possibility of salvation for non-Christians is a Christian possibility, since there is no other salvation apart from Christ. But how is it possible for the historical Jesus of Nazareth—his incarnation, crucifixion, and resurrection—to bring about salvation in a pre-Christian or extra-Christian context?

Rahner has dealt with this question in his discussion of Jesus' mediation of salvation. What is the horizon of transcendental understanding from which our insight into Christ's function as a mediator of salvation is acquired and which can be protected against misunderstandings, he asks. What is the inevitable experience on the horizon of which the unique historical event of the redeeming death of Jesus Christ comes to us and can be believed by us? This question of the mediation of Jesus is made particularly pressing because of the problem of anonymous Christianity. I can and indeed must ask myself, as a Christian, what this unique historical action performed by Christ has to do with me and how it can be my salvation. This question is, after all, ultimately the question as to what forms the special link uniting men to each other and to Christ.

On the basis of both scientific and theological consideration, Rahner does not give very much serious thought to the early teaching attributing the bond uniting all men to their common physical descent from the one parent, Adam, in paradise. He replaces this monogenetical unity of mankind by a unity based on man's historicity and his intercommunicative existence. If salvation plays a necessary constitutive part in human existence, he insists, intercommunication is an indispensable aspect of that existence in salvation or its absence. The question that has to be asked in this context, then, is how the grace of God is mediated in history and by 'mediated' here we mean, in the first place, 'offered'.

Man's association with his fellow men always results in a mediation of salvation—or disaster—because every time man accepts the offer of God's grace, that grace is made visible, since it contains God's revelation and his claim. As Rahner himself has said, whenever salvation takes place in the history of an individual's salvation, it acts as a mediation of salvation for all other men. Whenever a man believes, hopes, and loves, his faith, hope, and love have to become visible in word and deed, and that man is at the same time also the one who mediates God's salvation categorially. It is in this way that God offers himself to man and in this way that God's call is mediated categorially, a call to which man has to reply in freedom.

This is the mediated immediacy of man to God that takes place in categorial revelation. What it points to primarily is the sphere of understanding for an insight into saving significance of historical events as such. Rahner has found access to the more particular significance of the unique historical event of Jesus Christ in a process of thought that is based on the fact that human history itself reaches its climax in the incarnation, crucifixion, and resurrection of Jesus of Nazareth. His comment on this climax is that, because the world is one and God communicates himself to it in his Pneuma, it has, as history, only one aim and that is Jesus Christ.

It is correct to say that there were grace, justification, and the Spirit even before the coming of Christ, that all salvation has been given with regard to the merits of Jesus and that the event of Christ does not constitute the sole basis for the will of God to save, but is the expression and the effect of that will. These traditional explanations are not wrong, Rahner thinks, but they do not make it sufficiently clear what effect the incarnation and crucifixion of Christ have on the pre-Christian and extra-Christian possibility of salvation of non-Christians and how this is also able to be Christian. We cannot escape these difficulties and others that are not named, but very similar, if we think of the incarnation and crucifixion as what was known in scholastic theology as a 'final cause' of God's universal communication of himself that is present in his will to save. (In this context, Rahner says that the latter is called the 'Holy Spirit'.[49])

What does this mean? It means that, if the history of mankind as a whole has an aim that is given and brought about by God and if this aim includes a dynamic orientation of history in which history is in this sense determined, then the pre-Christian and extra-Christian history of man, both collectively and individually, is already determined by its end, which is given in the incarnation, crucifixion, and resurrection of Jesus Christ.

In this context, Rahner has made use of the concept of the 'seeking memory', by which he means that, wherever there is faith, hope, and love, faith is related to the eschatological completion of history that will take place in Jesus Christ. Man has the task of seeking in history and looking forward to its completion. He anticipates that end in the (anonymous) expression of his faith. The pre-Christian and the extra-Christian man cannot, of course, know the form that this completion of history will take, but it is the special characteristic of a final cause that it brings about here and now, by, as it were, transforming time, as what has still to come and is anticipated, something that is clear to everybody who to some extent understands the concept of the final cause. If this is in fact the case, then it should be possible to understand that in that faith, including pre-Christian and extra-Christian faith, this faith is itself made possible by the aim of this faith. To express this in a more concrete way, we can say that salvation is brought about by the incarnation, crucifixion, and resurrection of Jesus Christ because the believer—even if he is an anonymous Christian—seeks this eschatological completion of his faith, gives his consent to it and is for this reason given the power to believe, hope, and love. Despite the brevity and fragmentary nature of this outline, then, it should be clear that we may and indeed must call man's pre-Christian and extra-Christian salvation an anonymous Christian salvation.

All this can be made even clearer in what Rahner has called the 'seeking' Christology, and he makes it quite explicit in his three appeals to this seeking Christology in every man. In these appeals, the significance of explicit

Christianity and the reference of anonymous Christianity to Christ coincide, since Rahner tries to demonstrate in them that what is sought in any case is found in Christ.[50]

The Unity of Transcendental and Categorial Revelation

So far in this chapter, I have emphasized the transcendental aspect of revelation as resulting from the supernatural existential factor in man. Since God has always wanted man to be saved, despite his sin, there is a transcendental revelation of God and this is a revelation to *all* men. I stressed, in the case of man's transcendental experiences, that they are not necessarily explicitly or consciously known. The same applies to this transcendental revelation made to man. It is not a reality that man can make known to himself as something that is explicit by sinking down into his innermost self. This transcendental revelation of God is, on the contrary, always an aspect of the categorial revelation, in other words, of the revelation that is made visible, perceptible and objective and is articulated in history. This transcendental revelation is the necessary background to the categorial revelation and is expressed in the categorial revelation.

Whenever Rahner speaks of a revelation of God, then, both these aspects should be seen as forming constitutive elements of the one revelation. His division of revelation into a transcendental and a categorial revelation is therefore no more than a subsequent reflection about the one event of the God who reveals himself. In this reflection, an analysis is made of what forms a concrete and indissoluble unity in the reality of life. This unity existing between the transcendental and the categorial aspects of the one revelation of God cannot be overemphasized, since without it Rahner's teaching about revelation will be misunderstood or not understood at all. He has himself said that the event of revelation always has an element of supernaturally raised transcendence as its permanent and active existential factor in man. This transcendental experience of the absolute closeness of God is one aspect of the revelation of God, according to Rahner, and it cannot always be made objective in the case of every man. It is necessary for the real possibility of salvation of the non-Christian and it is also necessary if man is to believe the word of revelation at all. In this sense, then, it is a presupposition for man's knowledge of revelation as such.

The second aspect of this event of revelation is what Rahner has called its historical mediation or its objectivization in a supernaturally transcendental experience which occurs in history and as a whole even constitutes the whole of history. Within this one history of mankind, which, because the transcendental revelation of God has to be interpreted in history, is always a history of salvation and revelation and is therefore co-extensive with the whole history of mankind, Rahner has made a distinction between a more or less successful interpretation of the transcendental revelation in the non-Christian religions and philosophies on the one hand and the absolute, irrevocable and irreversible historical interpretation of the revelation of God in Jesus Christ. What is revealed in the unique and definitive climax of this history of revelation is the absolute and irrevocable unity of God's transcendental communication of himself to mankind and its historical mediation in a God-man, Rahner says with unambiguous clarity and then goes on to stress that this God-man is God himself as communicated to man, the human acceptance of that communication and the definitive appearance of that acceptance in one person.

This statement by Rahner about the God-man is of particular importance because it contains in a short and striking form precisely those elements which characterize the unity that exists between transcendental and categorial revelation. God communicates himself to man in the transcendental revelation and raising up of man. Man accepts this communication by responding freely and in dialogue to God's offer in faith, hope, and love and in this way achieves salvation. Finally, this acceptance of God's supernatural offer of salvation to man is automatically and inevitably also the spatio-temporal, historical appearance of the revelation that takes place in word and deed,[51] with the result that God's revelation cannot simply remain hidden in man's transcendentality, but has to appear. It has to become historical; this means that it becomes visible in the lives of men and is expressed objectively in reflective statements.

It is, however, possible that man may also—and perhaps necessarily—encounter God's revelation categorially precisely at that point where the transcendental revelation of God is interpreted historically in and via man. This has led Rahner to provide a Christological approach of a kind that has hardly been found in theology before. From all that we have seen so far, it should be clear that one of Rahner's most persistent concerns has always been to remove the suspicion of mythology from faith in the God who became man, since it hardly needs to be stressed that modern man is particularly inclined to attribute mythology to the teaching of Christian faith, especially in the doctrine of the incarnation. There are examples of phenomena that are similar to an incarnation in other religions—an obvious one being that of the Dalai Lama. Despite the definition of Chalcedon, the Christian can easily have the impression that Jesus behaved in a purely human fashion and that he assumed the form of a man as a kind of uniform that he could take off at any time. It has been one of Rahner's constant preoccupations to try to refute this belief of modern man in order to safeguard the credibility of Christian faith.

Prophets as Interpreters of the Transcendental Revelation

Rahner's point of departure for this approach to the mystery of Christ is the religion of the Old Testament in particular. In general, however, he finds this point of departure in all religions and claims that every person and every religion attempts to objectivize the transcendental revelation of God and to express that revelation, with the result that a partial expression at least of authentic, categorial revelation is contained in each religion.

Rahner is also aware of man's social structure and knows that every man is always deeply embedded in a particular culture with its own norms, values, modes of behaviour, and religious and philosophical ideas. He leaves it to those who specialize in comparative religion to examine the structure of these cultures and to explain why they have come about and how they function, but he has always stressed one aspect of this phenomenon that has a special bearing on the whole question of transcendental revelation. This is the particular function of the bearers of revelation or prophets. These he defines as those men who are entrusted with the task of bringing religion about and developing it. They may be individual founders of religions or philosophies, they may be reformers or they may be simply men whose words and actions result in certain impulses of a religious or related kind. He recently called the prophet the believer who is able to express his transcendental experience in the right way. Unlike other believers, he can express this experience in such a way that it is an objectivization of others' own transcendental experience of God and can be recognized by them as correct and convincing.

It is, therefore, not surprising that there should always be such people who can experience these transcendental moments, and express them better than we can, in words and actions. Rahner is not suggesting anything exceptional in

claiming that there are men who are, from the religious
point of view, especially gifted. These men live inspired by a
special and more intense experience of God and are more
clearly aware of the presence of God and the demands that
he makes at a given time and in a given situation. They know
this for themselves and can, moreover, articulate this
conviction in such a way that others are roused by their
words and deeds.

The message—the Christian message, for example, proclaimed in preaching—has a decisive effect when it is an
objectivization of an authentic experience of God addressed
to people who, on the basis of their transcendental structure, are already looking out, searching and waiting for this
word to which their innermost longings, which they may
find difficult to express in words or which may have become
stifled by tradition or the religious institution to which they
belong, can respond. The prophet or the bearer of revelation, then, must have not only a more intense than average
transcendental experience, but also a greater linguistic
facility. Rahner believes that self-expression of this kind,
that is successful and is given a really vital form, occurs in
the case of prophets and others so that their experiences
and their expression of those experiences can be a produc-
tive source of strength, an example and a norm for others.

From this point—that of prophets in general in the
history of comparative religions and of Old Testament
prophets in particular—it is possible to trace a line to the last
of the prophets and the bringer of salvation who was so
immersed in God that his words and actions were an
insurpassable expression of God himself in history. It is in
this way, then, that Rahner has developed his approach to
Jesus Christ and we shall have more to say about his ideas in
this respect later in the next chapter, which is devoted to his
Christology. For the time being, however, it should be noted
that his teaching about Jesus as the last prophet and the

absolute bringer of salvation is the same, in his view, as the Chalcedonian formula of the one divine person in two natures. He regards—correctly, in my opinion—his terminology as more readily accessible for contemporary man and believes that, if contemporary man is to be brought to an understanding of the incarnation of God at all, it can only be in his or a related way. I shall, however, consider Rahner's Christology separately in the next chapter. In the meantime, all that we have to bear in mind is that his Christological approach is, like all his theology, an anthropological approach.

I think that I have set out in this chapter the way in which Rahner views the development of religions in general and the way in which he evaluates them in the light of a Christian understanding of faith. To summarize, we may add that religions and philosophies or world-views arise in the first place from the inner dynamism of man's spirituality as manifested in his transcendental experiences.[52] We have, after all, to ask ourselves again and again: What really takes place when a person achieves his Christian salvation in an anonymous way? That person believes, hopes, and loves, but it is obvious that faith, hope, and love cannot simply remain enclosed within man's transcendental subjectivity. They must become historical, tangible and categorial. There are two well-known reasons for this and we shall conclude this section with a brief review of them.

In the first place, man only has transcendental experiences by reflecting about them or by associating with the categorial objects of his world in such a way that he is able to discover the transcendental aspect in them. Primarily, however, he acts and lives on the basis of the inner dynamism of his spirituality. This means that, by achieving his salvation, man makes the transcendental and supernatural aspect of his spirituality categorial in what he says and does. This in turn means that man is spirituality that is inseparably united to the body and that his spirituality is itself mediated via his own spatio-temporal corporeality. He can, in other words, only know in this way who and what he is. We may therefore conclude by saying that man's faith, hope, and love are all inevitably expressed in the categorial and material spatio-temporality of his existence.

In the second place, it should be borne in mind that man is bound to try to give a name to the ultimate destiny and the origin of his experiences. He wants to know what is true and to give a higher meaning to his life. He wants to be able to name his longing for total happiness and his experience of infinite promise. He wants to live for something that is worth the risk of failure. Because of this, he is almost driven to accept the idea of God or gods, the idea, at least, of a reality that he is on the one hand seeking, but that he cannot, on the other hand, find in the world.

To summarize these two aspects we may say that, in achieving his salvation in faith, hope, and love, man does not do this exclusively in explicit religiosity. He achieves salvation primarily by expressing his acceptance of his transcendental experience and living his everyday life in the light of that acceptance and by loving, trusting, hoping, working, caring, and persisting in thanksgiving.

The Non-Christian Religions

I have already said, at least implicitly, that, since the prophet has a special function in religion and not every man is a prophet, the categorial interpretation of transcendental revelation made to man in his religion is already present in all the known plausibility-structures. It also has to be borne in mind that the individual ought to have the possibility of participating in an authentic relationship with God in his life and that this relationship, which leads to man's salvation, should be present at all times and in all situations in the history of mankind. In the past, man was far more radically associated with his fellow men and had far closer bonds with society. It is therefore unthinkable that this relationship with God, which was made possible for him by God himself so that he might be saved, should have been available to him in a purely private and interior form, dissociated from the religion of the environment in which he was living. It is Rahner's deep conviction that man must have this positive relationship with God that saves him within the religion that is in fact available to him as an aspect of his environment. He regards it as a dangerous misconception from which we ought to free ourselves, if we confront a religion outside Christianity with the dilemma either of tracing all its positive teachings back to God and his will or of being no more than a human invention.

Rahner's conviction is derived from the fact that the religion of the Old Testament was based on divine revelation, but was not free of error and false interpretations. He has said about all religions that they all represent attempts made by men to mediate in reflection and objectively and to interpret the original unreflective and non-objective revelation. There are in all religions, he believes, individual aspects of successful mediation, made possible by God's grace, of man's supernaturally transcendent relationship with God. God has, however, allowed human guilt and this has the effect of debasing and overshadowing all aspects of man's collective and social life. This is also the case in the history of man's objectivizing interpretation of God's revelation. This interpretation is only partially successful. It is always part of an unfinished history. It is mixed with error and contains obscurities. These determine the religious situation in which man is placed, Rahner believes.

I cannot, nor do I have to develop this any further here. There is also the question as to whether other religions have anything to teach Christianity, but this is not strictly relevant to our present consideration. What is particularly important in our present context is the re-assessment of the non-Christian religions that has taken place in Christian circles. These religions are now rightly regarded, not exclusively perhaps, but quite certainly as God's revelation, because, as Rahner has claimed, man experiences in them the fact that he has been supernaturally raised up and finalized and he attempts to express this experience in words. A Christian is only able to distinguish the individual elements in these non-Christian religions that are right or wrong, valuable or harmful and positive or negative in the light of his Christian faith. Rahner's fundamental argument is that the whole history of mankind is at the same time a history of revelation.

God's Revelation of Himself Can Be Known

This last section of this chapter is both an addition to what I said previously in Chapter 4 about the possibility of faith in revelation, and an anticipation of what will be said about Rahner's Christology in the following chapter. Man can only ever have a relationship of mediated immediacy with God, according to Rahner. By this, he means that I can only be addressed and claimed by God and his redeeming word in the spatio-temporality of my own history or individual existence. At the same time, however, this claim must be known as a claim by God. God's revelation can be known, what is more, precisely as a divine revelation, even though it can never be grasped directly as such, but can only be understood in the categorial objectivizations of man's own world. These must be transparent so that God is able to reveal himself in them.

Rahner recognizes that this is a major problem of faith for modern man, who asks. How can I know God's revelation as such, if its coming to me is always mediated, in my reflection, in the message or activity of the prophet, or in the interpretation of other men? It is not possible, in our present context, to be concerned with the specific difficulty of the Christian's religiosity, but we can agree with what Rahner has said recently about another, related difficulty, that of how God and his activity are to be known in our concrete historical experience of the world. We cannot, he says, encounter God as an inexpressible mystery, as the ground of being or as the incomprehensible presupposition in our world. It seems as though he is unable to penetrate into the world with which we are associated because he wants, in this way, to be what he is not—an individual being, alongside whom there is something else that he is not. If it was his intention to appear in his world, he would, so it seems, at once cease to be himself, that is, the ground of all appearance who is and has no appearance. By definition, God seems to be unable to be within the world. It is, of course, possible to say hastily that it is not necessary for God to be in the world and that he must be regarded as being above the world. This, however, points to the fact that we have probably not even been aware of this radical difficulty. The difficulty, Rahner stresses, is to be found in the fact that God does not appear, by definition, to be able to be where we, by definition, are. Every objectivization of God that appears as a phenomenon in time and space, here and now, at the same time seems to be essentially not God, but something that can, as a phenomenon, be derived from other phenomena that can be postulated or defined within the categories of this world.

In the light of this difficulty, we are bound to ask once again: How can I know God's revelation as such? In the first place, of course, we as Christians are concerned with how God can be known in the interpretation of Jesus of Nazareth in signs, word, and deed. The question is not whether Jesus of Nazareth gave us in his life and teaching an exemplary relationship with God as a man, as so many people today think. The really decisive question is whether I am able to know whether God has really expressed himself in his most distinctive being and in his revelation of himself in Jesus of Nazareth in such a way that I have to do with the man Jesus' understanding of himself and of God and also that I am confronted with the revelation of God's word, in other words, with God's categorial revelation which calls on me to consent in freedom and faith.

This is only possible on the basis of what Rahner calls an analogous experience between the transcendental (and therefore universally human) revelation and its categorial (and therefore spatio-temporal and historical) interpretation and appearance.[53] There is no compulsion in this analogous experience. It calls for the freedom of moral decision. It is faith, but faith that has to be justified in the light of reason. (Rahner is quite aware that faith in Jesus Christ may be refused—and usually is refused—for different reasons from those of the stupidity or malice of the one who cannot accept that faith.) With reference to the Old Testament revelation, Rahner has said that it is not the concrete content of this history before the time of Christ in the old covenant that makes it a history of revelation, since, from the categorial point of view, nothing happens in it that does not happen in any other history of a people. It is, he thinks, the interpretation of this history as a partnership in dialogue with God and as a tendency towards the open future that makes it a history of revelation. This can only mean that there is a history of revelation in the old covenant because Israel was conscious that it was directly addressed by God in the categorial events of its history, that were very similar to those occurring in the history of other peoples and interpreted those events as part of a partnership in dialogue with God. I can therefore only understand categorial events as God's call if they take place in a definite (religious) context and make it possible for me to have an analogous experience.

On the basis of these presuppositions, then, we may go on to ask whether it is not possible for there to be a real divine revelation in mediated immediacy in the religions of other peoples in addition to the Old Testament revelation, and whether the categorial revelation of the word, in analogy with the Old Testament, as temporary and replaceable, does not take place everywhere whenever man asks systematic and explicit questions about God. Rahner's reply to these questions is 'yes', arguing that, in achieving salvation, man provides a historical interpretation of his supernaturally transcendental consciousness, first in his activity and then in the explicit expression of religious doctrines and dogma. God is, according to Rahner, active in this process. If he were not, there could not be any supernatural salvation. The result of this is that man's religious interpretation of his world can never be simply a natural interpretation carried out by man, in which the subject is himself or his world—it must represent the way in which God reveals himself in the world, that is, in the manner of mediated immediacy, in which man knows that he really encounters a statement and a claim made by God in a man's interpretation of himself and in his words and actions. To use Rahner's own terminology, what takes place in such a case is a categorial revelation or God's revelation of his word.

Rahner's transcendental approach is universal, and for this reason, as far as the concept of revelation is concerned, it is always exposed to the danger of not having a clear view of the categorial aspect of one reality and seeing it sufficiently explicitly and in accordance with its real meaning. Assuming the existence of man's supernatural existential factor, it is therefore possible to say that the revelation of God is present when God turns to me in a free relationship of dialogue in the word and deed of another human being, in other words, in mediated immediacy. That revelation also exists, for example, when I am addressed by another person as though directly by God. It is also present when I experience something of God's love and nearness, something that would otherwise always be closed to me even though I might know, on the basis of transcendental revelation, that the statements made by the prophet are not so strange and do not appear as completely different from my own inner dynamism. God's categorial revelation is not a statement about God derived from my own innermost being. There is a history of God with man and this is not always the same either from God's side or from man's.

Whenever a man consigns himself in a radical movement of self-deification to the transcendental ground of his being, his words and actions become an ultimate and unsurpassable revelation of God. In such a case, that man's history makes God visible in a categorial reality that cannot be superseded, but, at the same time, cannot be theoretically traced back to anyone who does not hand himself over in this way. In spite of God's transcendental revelation, which inevitably implies at least a partially successful revelation of the word, there is still sufficient room for the absolute bringer of salvation and the last of the prophets. I can only continue to hope that I shall hear the categorial reality of God as though it were communicated by him. Those who specialize in comparative religion are right in their assertion that, from the human point of view at least, all religions are fragmentary attempts to express the inexpressible and to determine what cannot be defined. According to Rahner, these attempts are not always and not necessarily false, but they are no more than attempts. One religion is no more correct than the others. The possibility of distinguishing is only present if one believes in the one who was so filled with God and so open as a human being to the infinite reality that God himself and his plan to save men were so manifest in that man that the divine reality appeared in the human reality without being distorted by it.

In the following chapter, I shall try to show that it is possible to believe in that man, Jesus of Nazareth, since, as Rahner has pointed out in *Christian at the Crossroads,* everything that has been said about God and man's experience of God, about transcendental revelation and historical interpretation and about man's longings and fears 'is mysteriously synthesized in the encounter with Jesus of Nazareth. In this synthesis, man's hope and experience of Jesus support each other in an indissoluble circle and operate as a mutual justification in man's conscience with an intellectual honesty that expresses itself in what Christians call humility'.

·6·

'I believe in Jesus Christ'

This is the title of one of Rahner's theological medita-
tions. Part of a series of sermons given in Münster, it
expresses in a concise and dynamic way the most important
aspects of Rahner's faith in Jesus Christ.[54] His concern in
this respect can be expressed by continuing the thought
begun at the end of the preceding chapter: All men have
transcendental experiences and therefore an inner dynamism, which Rahner, for theological reasons, ascribes to the
supernatural, divine order of being. Man transcends himself
by virtue of God's communication of himself in grace and
man's transcendentality is oriented towards something that
he cannot possess or find in the world. All that is present
categorially within the world is a promise of something
greater because man cannot imagine—in words or
concepts—anything that cannot be transcended. Nonetheless, this inner dynamism is still given primarily, that is,
apart from inadequate reflection, in the transcendental
consciousnes. What, then, is the intention of this dynamism?

I touched on this question when I discussed anonymous
Christianity in the previous chapter. In the first place, this
dynamism aims at a tangible, historical and therefore
spatio-temporal assurance of the fact that life is meaningful
and valuable and that all the care and anxiety, suffering and
pain on the one hand and happiness, love, faithfulness and
thanksgiving on the other are not simply passing moments

that will cease to exist when life ceases and death takes over. It looks, in other words, for an assurance of the hope that man has. To quote once more from Rahner's *Christian at the Crossroads*: 'What is the relationship between this incomprehensible mystery of our life and ourselves? Is it always in the eternally unattainable distance? Will it always be a question that can only be answered in the light of itself, but will always remain silent? Will the infinite and infinitely distant future ever become the present? Will the abyss ever become a home that offers shelter and security, our definitive homeland? Is there a forgiveness that is able to put an end to a guilt that cannot be overcome by itself?'

As we have seen at the end of the previous chapter, Rahner believes that all these questions expressing man's experience of his own existence and his spiritual dynamism are 'mysteriously synthesized in the encounter with Jesus of Nazareth'. This means that Jesus of Nazareth is, for Rahner, the answer to the question that man of necessity asks and the openness that man must be. Of course, if Jesus Christ is to be that answer, man must allow these transcendental questions to come to him, since, if he has no questions, he will receive no answer.

It is possible to say that everything that we have said about Rahner so far—the whole of his theology as outlined in the earlier part of this book—is important in itself, but is really ultimately a preparation for the essential Christological problem. In his brief presentation of Rahner's Christology, Arno Schilson has said: 'The fate of Rahner's transcendental Christology will be decided at this point—the possibility of an immediate experience of God as the mystery that embraces all things. If it is indeed possible to approach his Christology in this way, it will retain its value and develop its potential. If, on the other hand, it remains questionable, it will, in the long run, not prove valuable.'[55]

Rahner would probably dispute Schilson's last statement

and say that the immediate experience of God cannot be questionable, since, if it were, man would cease to be human. Probably what Schilson means is that it is possible for the transcendental questions that arise as a result of man's (transcendental) experience of God to be thrust into the background and therefore not sufficiently subjected to reflection. What may happen under certain circumstances is that we may approach the crucial questions with a sceptical attitude and not ask them because we do not expect a satisfactory answer. This, of course, is why Rahner has taken such pains to prove that man's transcendental experiences are experiences of God and why these experiences play such an important part in his theology. The encounter with Jesus of Nazareth therefore synthesizes these experiences and the questions arising from them and, as Rahner has said, this synthesis has to be justified 'with an intellectual honesty that expresses itself in what Christians call humility'.

It is worth considering in this context the problem underlying this claim of Rahner's. If Jesus is the absolute bringer of salvation (a fact that we shall try to establish later) and if I believe in Jesus Christ, the question that arises is: Why should it be Jesus Christ? Why am I concerned precisely with him and not with the many other founders of religions or prophets?

Rahner has also asked this question in the theological meditation, the title of which forms the heading to this chapter (pp. 32–34): 'We should not make too high demands when we first approach the question why Jesus and only Jesus represents this human reality. Ideas, theories and reflections about God are, of course, necessary, but they are of secondary importance. They are only one aspect of the primary process. Man's true encounter with God occurs in history. I therefore have the right and the duty to look out in history for a concrete encounter with the decisive answer made by God about my existence. And even if that answer cannot be found, it is still necessary to go on looking for it, not as an abstract idea, but as a future reality. If we look in this way and do not believe that it must inevitably always be the same in history and—because this reality has to be sought in the future—it will never be found in the present as the fulfilment of hope, then it is not too difficult to know that Jesus is the ultimate and unique concrete encounter with God'. Rahner concludes this statement with several important questions about the position of Jesus Christ in history: 'Where is there another man in history who would have made a claim to this event as having taken place in him? Where is there a man whose human life, death, and resurrection and whose being loved by countless people can give the courage and justification to leave themselves unconditionally to him, apart from the Jesus of the Bible?'

This is one answer that Rahner has given to the question: 'Why should it be Jesus Christ?' He has also given another reason, based on the fact that, when he reflects about himself and his faith, a man can simply begin with what he is and what he already believes. The limited nature of his existence makes it fundamentally impossible for him to work his way through every possible religion and philosophy. Why should he not begin, then, with the one who was the only one in history to assert that he was more than simply a prophet and to claim that he was himself the self-communication of God to man. He would have done what was required by his conscience in accordance with the demands of intellectual honesty if this claim were justified in a full discussion about the historical Jesus. He ought not to reject this claim in an attitude of scepticism and distrust. Even though he may know, subconsciously perhaps, that he has not reflected enough about his Christian faith and that there may be religions or world-views which make the same claims of truth as the Christian religion, he has nonetheless to take the risk. As a result of this, Rahner has asked two more closely related questions. The first is: What is the claim made by the historical Jesus of Nazareth and is this claim justified? The second is: How can modern man be given a correct understanding of the God-man that is free from all suspicion of mythology? In the sections that follow, I shall consider both these questions carefully. For convenience, I shall examine the first question in the section that follows immediately, on the claim of this historical Jesus. In the subsequent section, I shall look at the second question, in which an outline is given of Rahner's transcendental Christology.

The Claim of the Historical Jesus

Rahner has said recently that, according to Christian teaching, historical events that occurred in the distant past continue to affect our existence and at the same time contain within themselves an element of uncertainty, doubtfulness, and controversy that is inevitable and insuperable. Rahner has called this the fundamental difficulty experienced by modern man in connection with the claim of the historical Jesus. This difficulty is also connected with the exegesis of the New Testament, because we are bound to ask whether the contents are reliable.

Before I attempt to answer Rahner's question about the reliability of the claim of Jesus, I must say something about his attitude towards biblical exegesis. In the first place, he hardly ever quotes texts from the Old or New Testaments in order to prove his own claims. This is so for various reasons. For one, he does not want to give the impression that he is himself an exegete, since he has no specialized knowledge of biblical studies. Furthermore, he clearly hopes that he has absorbed enough of the methods and findings of modern biblical theology to be able to make use of them in his transcendental theology.

He has, in fact, often been criticized for making too little use of recent exegesis. This may be true, but it is equally true to say that he displays a remarkable knowledge of modern biblical research whenever he does apply it to his dogmatic theology, though it cannot be denied that his relationships with exegetes are not untroubled. He has more than once accused them of leaving the task of building a bridge between exegesis and dogmatic theology to the dogmatic theologians, who have done this job as best they could, but in the end have always had to go back to the exegetes, since every bridge has foundations on both banks of the river. At the same time, he has not resisted saying publicly that exegetes are fond of declaring that dogmatic theologians understand nothing of exegesis and carry it out very clumsily—so badly in fact that they ought not to do it at all. Who, then, should? Rahner has noted the strange impression made by exegetes, who complain that dogmatic theologians pay too little attention to Scripture and biblical theology and concentrate almost exclusively on scholasticism, while making excuses as soon as they are asked to provide evidence for the basis in Scripture of the Church's teachings and insisting that, with the best will in the world, nothing at all can be found in the Bible to support, for example, certain sacramental or Mariological dogmas. According to Rahner, exegetes have the habit of saying that such teachings are justified only by the Church's magisterium and tradition. He believes too that exegetes are often to blame indirectly for the excessive verbosity of many dogmatic theologians, since they do not supply the latter with the biblical evidence that they need for truths of the Catholic faith.

Why has Rahner reproached exegetes in this way? It is, I think, because his creative theological work has all been done at a time when Catholic exegetes have been—fortunately—departing from the traditional Catholic interpretation of Scripture and the Church's tradition no longer sets the norm for exegetical praxis. This has—unfortunately perhaps—frequently led to mutually irreconcilable interpretations within scriptural exegesis and, in the case of Christology, it is seldom possible to say with any certainty which statements can be attributed to the historical Jesus and which can 'only' be ascribed to the theology of faith of the early Church. Rahner therefore—not simply because he is not a professional exegete—confines himself in the question of the claim of the historical Jesus to minimal statements, in which there is no dispute that more can be derived from scriptural sources than simply these minimal statements themselves.

That, then, is Rahner's answer. He refuses to be confronted with the dilemma that a report must either be believed in all its details or else simply rejected. The Gospels, he knows, are not biographies. They were formed by the faith and Easter experience of the disciples. This does not, however, necessarily mean that there are objections to a justification of our knowledge of the claim of the historical Jesus. In the first place, Rahner has pointed out that Jesus did not regard himself simply as one of the many prophets in a line that was always open. On the contrary, he saw himself, Rahner insists, as the eschatological prophet and absolute and definitive bringer of salvation. In the second place, we are, according to Rahner, able to believe in Jesus' claim if we look, from the point of view of our transcendental experience of God's absolute communication of himself, in faith at the event mediated by the bringer of salvation in the whole of his real existence—the resurrection of Jesus. If these two arguments can be confirmed, Rahner has said, everything that has to be achieved in the interests of fundamental theology will have been done and all the other statements about Jesus as the Christ can be left to faith alone.

It should be clear from this last comment that Rahner

does not regard the resurrection of Jesus simply as one miracle alongside others, but as the ultimate confirmation of everything that Jesus claimed to be during his earthly life. The significance of the resurrection event should not, in his opinion, simply be derived from our contemporary understanding of events. On the contrary, the resurrection should be understood as it must have been understood by Jewish believers of the period—as the beginning, or as the end of time that had already begun.

There have also been other questions about the historical Jesus to which Rahner has provided striking answers. One of these is the question of Jesus' knowledge and his consciousness of himself. Rahner has shown that, although he was God made man, Jesus was not omniscient, despite the attempts made by a movement of popular piety in Christianity to prove that he was. If he were omniscient, Rahner asks, what would remain of his humanity? A distinction had to be made in the case of Jesus between a transcendental, non-objective knowledge, in which he was seen to be with God in a unique way, and an objective and concrete knowledge that he had as a man.

Rahner has pointed out recently that, despite a profound consciousness of his radical and unique nearness to God which persisted throughout the whole of his life (this sense of nearness is reflected in his special relationship with the 'Father'), Jesus had a knowledge which was objectivizing and verbalizing and which was at the same time also deeply conditioned by historical and social factors, having everything in common with the sphere of understanding and the concepts of his environment. This influence of his environment applied to his consciousness of himself and was not simply a condescension towards others. In this self-consciousness, he learned, had new and surprising experiences, and was threatened by crises of self-identification which, without being in any way less severe in their effects, were nonetheless protected by the knowledge that they were secure in the Father's will. All that we can call reliable here are what Rahner himself regards as those aspects of our historical knowledge of Jesus, in other words, the minimal statements that are valid for the historical Jesus. What, then, are these minimal statements? Rahner has reduced them to six.

First, Jesus lived in the religious environment of his own people, that is, within the already existing historical situation in which he found himself, and accepted all its aspects—the religious life, the synagogue, the feasts, customs, laws, priests, teachers, scriptures, the Temple, and so on—as legitimate and as required by God. He was a religious reformer and not a radical religious revolutionary. The extent to which his message and his interpretation of his religious background and environment does in fact constitute a radical 'revolution' is a different question.

Second, leading on from this first point, Rahner recognizes that, as a radical reformer, Jesus broke through the monopoly of the Jewish law which had set itself up in place of God. (This was not, of course, the original intention of the Mosaic law and it was not interpreted in this way by Paul.) Jesus opposed legalism, both in the form of pious ethics and in that of a justice based on works which aimed to protect man against God. He was conscious of his nearness to God, whom he regarded not as a mere cipher pointing to the significance of man, but as the ultimate reality. Because of this, he lived in solidarity with the social and religious outcasts of his environment, knowing that these were the people whom his Father loved. He resolutely accepted the struggle provoked by his attitude and activities on the part of the religious and social authorities. He did not, however, directly criticize society himself.

Third, although he hoped for success in his religious mission in the form of a conversion on the part of his own people, he became more and more convinced that his mission was leading him into fatal conflict with the religious and political establishment.

Fourth, he faced death with resolution, accepting it as the inevitable consequence of his faithfulness to his mission and as something that was imposed on him by the Father.

Fifth, he preached with reforming zeal to arouse men and call them back to God because of his consciousness of the nearness of the kingdom of God. At the same time, he also gathered disciples around him. These followed and 'imitated' him. The question that arises in this context is whether these disciples committed themselves to a matter that was, in the last resort, not directly connected with Jesus or whether that matter to which Jesus committed himself so completely, the matter of the immanent kingdom of God, was indissolubly associated with him. Jesus clearly did not consider the fact that he might only be followed in an explicitly socially critical commitment to the underprivileged and the oppressed. This negative observation does not imply that all human activity has no social relevance if it is not intended as such and that it only has this social relevance when it is intended as such, with the result that the whole theology of Jesus can be interpreted as 'political' theology.

Sixth and finally, from the historical point of view, a great many questions about Jesus' life and attitudes before the Easter event must inevitably remain open. Did he, for example, have a verbalized consciousness of his messianic mission? Which of the more than fifty names that he is given in the New Testament correspond most closely to his understanding of himself? Does the title given him by the Christological teaching of the New Testament itself, the 'Son of Man', form one of Jesus' *ipsissima verba* or can this not be established? Did Jesus, at least from time to time, perhaps think of a possible difference between himself and a future Son of Man? Did he, before the Easter event, explicitly ascribe a soteriological function to his death beyond that outlined above under the fourth point and, if so, to what extent did he do this and in what sense? Finally, did he, before the Easter event and in the imminent expectation of the kingdom of God, regard his disciples as a new community that had to be established and was already established? In what sense did he see them as the new Israel of those who believed in him? To what extent did he want this community to be institutionalized?

The above six points cover most aspects of Rahner's convictions with regard to our historical knowledge about Jesus' claim. At first sight it seems very little. They are, in fact, minimal statements, but they are sufficient for Rahner's purpose, which is primarily to familiarize modern man with the mystery of the God-man.

Rahner's Transcendental Christology

The definitive Chalcedonian formula of 451, defining the relationship between Jesus' divinity and humanity, has continued to be regarded throughout the centuries as a statement of a reality—God became man; the Word was made flesh—that cannot be expressed in any other way and cannot be replaced by another formulation. According to the definition of Chelcedon, 'Jesus Christ is at once complete in divinity and complete in humanity, truly God and truly man . . . consisting of two natures, without confusion, without change, without division, without separation; the distinction of natures being in no way annulled by the union but rather the characteristics of each nature being preserved and coming together to form one person and hypostasis'.[56]

It is only quite recently that attempts have been made to express this mystery of the incarnation of God in a new way that may be more readily intelligible to modern man than the earlier biblical and Hellenistic formulations. This does

not mean that the scriptural or the Chalcedonian statements
cease to be valid. Rahner has recognized, however, that, if it
was possible to translate, as it were, the mystery of the
incarnation into words, Chalcedon can surely not be the
end. It is indeed not the last word, but an invitation to begin
again. In this section, we shall consider Rahner's new
beginning in Christology, commencing with a brief survey
of the difficulties that confront contemporary man in his
understanding of this dogma.

The first difficulty has been mentioned before in this
book—the danger of a mythological misunderstanding
(there are, after all, incarnations in almost all religions) and
the closely connected idea that is encountered equally
frequently of God's apparent humanity. Rahner himself has
spoken of God appearing in the uniform of a human nature
which only clings to him externally and putting things right
on earth because he could no longer do it from heaven or of
God behaving in a human way in Jesus Christ without any
sense really being what we all are. He has therefore called
for a translation of ontic Christology, that is, a Christology
expressed in terms of nature, person, God-man, and so on,
into an ontological Christology. He has himself defined the
latter as a Christology in which the 'nature' to be assumed is
not understood in advance and in the first approach to
conceptualization as an objective matter, but as a transcendental spirituality. Essence and being do not simply have
transcendence here, Rahner has pointed out—they *are*
transcendence. For this reason, it must be possible to
express the substantial unity with the Logos in the conceptualization of that transcendence and for this to be translated
into conceptualization, so that what is meant by the hypostatic union can be made quite clear and protected against a
mythological misinterpretation.

Christ did not, Rahner believes, simply assume human
nature like a thing through which God acts. The claim that

he became man must also be expressed and described from the point of view of the man Jesus of Nazareth if it is to be justified and shown to be true. The danger of a mythological misunderstanding of the incarnation can only be avoided, Rahner thinks, in a transcendental Christology which at the same time sets itself the task of establishing a background against which the mystery of the incarnation can be properly understood. He has insisted on the explicit necessity of a transcendental Christology which stresses the *a priori* possibilities in man for the reception of the message of Christ, especially at a time when it is no longer possible to ignore the claims of a transcendental anthropology in preference to an anthropology that can only be established empirically and described *a posteriori*.

Having discussed the difficulties that contemporary man experiences in connection with the incarnation, I can now proceed to consider what Rahner's transcendental Christology is, what its aims are and what it tries to achieve.

The Aim of Rahner's Transcendental Christology

Let us take as our point of departure Rahner's use of the word 'transcendental' in the context of 'Christology'. Why does Rahner speak about a 'transcendental' Christology, when the term 'transcendental' is more reminiscent of the subjective element in me and is less suitable for anything objective or to be applied to others.

Rahner has spoken of a transcendental deduction and has said that the question ought to be asked more explicitly than usual why man is the one who is able to believe in the Christ of the Christian dogma. What came later to be known as his transcendental Christology ought strictly speaking to be called a 'transcendentally deduced Christology'. The 'idea of Christ' can be gained from the *a priori* structure of man, since this is what Rahner has called a reflective coming to oneself of a religious *a priori* that is found in every Christian.

This 'idea of Christ' has therefore, according to Rahner, to be deduced from man's understanding of himself. It is not simply any idea in the sense of a thought that one may or may not have, but rather an idea that is necessarily present with man. This deduction, Rahner has said in the same context, ought to move in the direction that is indicated as follows. Man is at the same time a corporeal historical being of the earth and a being of absolute transcendence. He therefore looks out—in his history—to see whether he cannot find the highest fulfilment of his being and his expectations (however free it may remain) in which his concept of the absolute is filled (it will otherwise remain empty) and his way of seeing is made clear (he will otherwise remain blind) and both point in the direction of the absolute God. Man is therefore in this sense the one who can expect the free epiphany of God in his history. That epiphany is Jesus Christ.

We may say, then, with Rahner that the task of a transcendental Christology is to show that man expects, with an inner transcendental necessity, God's historical promise to be fulfilled in him. His reasons for hoping for this fulfilment should be clear from what we have said in the previous chapter. In history, he is looking for a place, Rahner has said, in which this bold act of hope is fulfilled in him. The point of departure for a transcendental Christology is therefore to be found in the experiences which man always has—even when he is protesting against them—and which, in the immediacy of their objects which are in the foreground and through which they are mediated, do not fulfil the claim to absolute fulfilment or salvation which man inevitably makes of them. In these transcendental experiences, the objects of this world—and especially of man's personal environment—are experienced as a promise of absolute fulfilment and also as an absolute claim, although this cannot be justified in the light of those objects alone.

What man is ultimately seeking, of course, is valid truth, the meaning and aim of his life, a reason for the hope that he cannot abandon, a possibility of becoming free from suffering and death and a justification of his love of God and his fellow men. These transcendental experiences, which cannot be given up and are in themselves inevitable and which make it possible for man to be truly human, confront man with questions which are important for him to answer. He therefore looks for an answer with concentrated urgency as the questions themselves arise. The questions themselves do not provide their own answers, even though man may hope, wish, and 'believe' in the profane sense of the word that all will somehow be well. Hope and expectation, even when they are suppressed, are not in any sense fulfilment. Only God can give this fulfilment (or not give it!) and it always of necessity takes place in history. Transcendental Christology therefore has the aim of reminding man that the 'idea of Christ' as Rahner calls it is necessary to him and that he must look for fulfilment in history. He is not that fulfilment and cannot be it.

This may give the impression that Rahner is postulating a transcendental deduction of the event of Christ from mankind. He has himself made it clear, however, that this is not so. It is not possible simply to deduce the 'idea of Christ' in whom everything finds its fulfilment,[57] nor can we say that an 'idea of Christ' has in fact been fulfilled in the historical Jesus of Nazareth. What is more, we cannot say, on the basis of the idea itself, how this fulfilment takes place. It may, for example, simply be the end of history. Assuming that history will continue, however, Rahner has pointed out, we can only establish on the basis of a consideration of the concrete life and resurrection of Jesus himself whether this fulfilment is in fact given with Jesus.

Rahner is above all conscious of the fact that even a transcendental Christology must be based on faith and has pointed out that it is only by reflecting about the experienced fact that we can perceive the transcendental possibility of the idea of Christ. He does not behave as though he were a non-Christian thinking about a transcendental Christology, which he naturally finds in Christ. This is why he has said again and again that our point of departure should always be faith as it is. This point of departure in our existing relationship with Jesus Christ is, in his opinion, fully justified from the human point of view and therefore also from the point of view of fundamental theology. It may well be necessary for a transcendental Christology to be based on the idea of an absolute bringer of salvation. The Christian may have to be accountable to himself and to others for a historical approach to the question. He may also be right in believing that Jesus was the absolute bringer of salvation. Despite all this, however, he should not behave as though he can and should establish a relationship in faith between man and Jesus Christ by means of such reflections. Transcendental Christology may have an apologetical function, but its primary aim is to show that man is oriented towards Jesus Christ and that he can find in Christ what he has always been looking for. This will become even clearer when we have considered what Rahner means by the 'idea of Christ'. To do this, it is necessary to examine the terms with which he defines that idea.

The Many Names of the One Jesus Christ

What strikes us if we go more deeply into Rahner's Christology is that it is not only in accordance with his anthropological approach, but also that he prefers the term 'absolute bringer of salvation', to the concept of 'incarnation'. He has even gone so far as to say that a transcendental Christology points essentially to an absolute bringer of salvation, which means that the 'idea of Christ' is not primarily described in ontic categories, but is also the basis of the function that

Jesus has for me personally and for humanity in general, a function of which Jesus himself was aware. According to whatever function he wishes to emphasize, Rahner varies the name, calling Jesus, in addition to the absolute bringer of salvation, the mediator of salvation, the last prophet, or the last of the prophets. He also speaks of the saving event, meaning Jesus Christ. He uses many adjectives to describe Jesus as the bringer of salvation. Why, then, does he use so many names, frequently qualifying them with descriptive adjectives?

I have already referred several times to Rahner's anxiety to avoid at all costs any suspicion of mythology that might be caused by the doctrine of the incarnation. His Christology, which he often calls a 'Christology from below', is therefore an approach made from the standpoint of man and his understanding of himself to an understanding of God's incarnation. The names and qualities which Rahner ascribes to Jesus Christ do not, it is true, necessarily arise from his transcendental theology, but Rahner's intention is still the same.

It is not difficult to understand the attributes that Rahner ascribes to the bringer of salvation if we recall for a moment his fundamental theological thesis, namely that man is essentially openness to the ultimate self-communication of God. The incarnation can be made intelligible to modern man precisely because of his essential openness. God's incarnation does not, however, take place in every man, even though every man is also, in his faith, hope and love, an expression of God's communication of himself and an attempt is made in every religion to objectivize this self-communication, an attempt that is partly successful. Because every man is, in this sense, a mediator of salvation for other men, the special position of Jesus as the bringer of salvation had to be emphasized.

The truth of the incarnation, Rahner has said, would

become mythological if it were simply a datum applying to each man. One fact that can easily be overlooked is that, in such a case, the humanity of God, in which he is the individual who is there for every individual man, cannot receive grace in itself with a nearness of God or an encounter with God that is essentially different from the only encounter with God in which he communicates himself and in which grace is given to every man. That encounter, of course, reaches its climax in man's beatific vision. (It may be worth pointing out that the *visio beatifica* is enjoyed by man in the hereafter. The *unio hypostatica* is the term first used by the Council of Chalcedon to express the mystery of Christ, in which the divine and the human natures of the divine person of Jesus exist in unity.) It is therefore not the case that God's communication of himself is the same in all men.

I have noted that Rahner believes that the Chalcedonian teaching can be expressed differently and, what is more, that it can be formulated in such a way that an attempt is made to approach it 'from below', that is, from man's point of view. If Rahner is right, then the bringer of salvation must inevitably be different from a special religious genius, one prophet among many or a mediator of salvation in the context of the universal human mediation of salvation. This, then, is why Rahner ascribes so many apparently stereotyped attributes to the bringer of salvation.

Rahner speaks of an absolute self-communication on the part of God, saying, in this context, that, with the exception of the beatific vision, God always expresses himself by a finite reality, a word or an event that belongs to the finite world of created reality. As long, however, as this finite mediation of God's self-expression does not represent a reality of God himself in the strict sense of the word, it will always be fundamentally temporary and surpassable, because it is finite and, in this finite state, not the reality of God himself. It can therefore, from the standpoint of God himself, be replaced by a new projection of the finite. God's communication of himself in Jesus Christ must therefore be brought into prominence, as it were, in contrast to a self-communication that is not absolute. If the reality of Jesus is in fact the unique, irreplaceable and definitive promise and acceptance, Rahner says, then we are bound to say that this reality is not simply something that has been brought about by God—it is God himself.

The real problem, then, is not only to be found at the level of knowledge, but also at the level of expression. The question arises therefore as to whether I am able to know God himself in a man and how I must describe that man in such a way that God himself is expressed in this expression. Rahner formulated this question in a most striking way when he described the reality of Jesus as not simply something brought about by God, but as God himself. He continues this idea by saying that, if this promise is itself a human reality as something that has received grace absolutely, and if this promise is absolutely God himself, it is the absolute belonging of a human reality to God, what we traditionally call the hypostatic union. This union is not different from our grace by what is promised in it, because this is in both cases grace (even in the case of Jesus), but by the fact that Jesus is this promise for us and we are not ourselves the promise, but the receivers of God's promise to us.

According to Rahner, the concept of the hypostatic union means this and nothing more than this: In this human possibility, Jesus, is the absolute will of God to save, the absolute event of God's communication of himself to us, as well as the acceptance of that self-communication as brought about by God himself and a reality of God himself, unadulterated, but also inseparable and therefore irrevocable.

If this statement is analyzed, what emerges is how a

bringer of salvation must be expressed and understood if he is the reality of God himself and if he not only says something about God, but also is the making visible of God himself in human history. What has to be said of the absolute bringer of salvation must also be made manifest and justified in Jesus' understanding of himself, in his death and resurrection. This only points once again to the fact that the idea of Christ or that of an absolute bringer of salvation cannot be deduced *a priori* and in fact makes an appeal to man's *a priori* understanding of himself. It also points to the fact that it is quite legitimate to have the real Christ in mind when a first approach is made to a transcendental Christology. We are therefore brought back again to the question: What qualities should be ascribed to a bringer of salvation so that, as a man, he is at the same time the reality and the self-expression of God?

Rahner has expressed himself quite clearly in this context. The proclamation must, he insists, be identical with the one who proclaims it; in other words, the one who announces the message must at the same time himself be the message, and in such a way that his promise of salvation to us cannot be separated from his person. The matter cannot be presented as though the Logos became man and simply said something of God's by speaking. As soon as we conceive the incarnation in this way, it becomes superfluous. This is because God could have had the words that the man Jesus said of him as the envoy of God said by any other prophet. The man Jesus must, Rahner stresses, as himself and not simply by his words, be God's revelation of himself.

Jesus is a prophet who does away with the function of the prophets by the claim made by his word, because his word is the unique, unrepeatable and ultimate word of God and he understood it in this sense and knew that this word was indissolubly linked with himself and his life, death, and resurrection. And not only his word, but also his whole fate is connected intimately with God. If we see Jesus in this way, Rahner thinks, it is no longer possible to separate what is proclaimed from the one who proclaims it or the humanity of Jesus from God—something that can and indeed has to be done in the case of all the other prophets. In this perspective, we can see that salvation is promised to us in a man and not simply in a 'word' that someone else might have said. It is given to us in the person of Jesus.

This, then, is the first point, namely that there is a close bond between God's revelation and the humanity of Jesus. It leads directly to Rahner's second point, which is that this bringer of salvation is God's irrevocable act for man. What later became known as a result of Jesus' rising from the dead, namely that the whole Jesus of Nazareth, including his humanity, was accepted by God in the resurrection, has to be assumed in advance here. A number of such assumptions are made in this context by Rahner. He presupposes, for example, that God is himself man and continues to be man in eternity. As a consequence, all theology will presumably continue to be anthropology in eternity. Man is forbidden to have a low opinion of himself, because this is the same as having a low opinion of God. If God is always a mystery, then man is also the mystery of God and will continue to be a mystery in eternity, sharing in the mystery of God as the ground of his being. God's act of salvation, achieved by the absolute bringer of salvation, is, Rahner believes, irrevocable, because God can never cease to be man.

We now come to the third point made by Rahner in this context. The event of salvation is irreversible, just as salvation itself is irrevocable, not merely temporary and not dependent on presuppositions or conditions of any kind, but absolute. It is in itself the fulfilment of salvation, to such a degree that, although it has been accomplished in an exemplary way in one man, the salvation of that one man is at the same time the possibility of salvation and indeed salvation itself for all men. The bringer of salvation, who forms the highest point in God's communication of himself to the world, must therefore be God's absolute promise to the spiritual creature, man, and at the same time the acceptance of God's communication of himself by the bringer of salvation. This is because, Rahner says, history cannot reach the stage of its irreversibility. It is only then that irrevocable self-communication takes place on both sides and is present in historical communication in the world.

The climax or the eschatological end of history is reached either when the history of mankind as a whole is discontinued in God or when the eschatological end takes place, in a continuing history, in a man and this saving event at the same time brings about salvation for all men. This eschatological saving event which occurred in Christ should not be regarded as absolute, at least in the sense that it is the same as the completion of mankind in the immediacy of the beatific vision, Rahner points out, since, if it were, history would already be at an end. It must be understood in the sense that the irreversibility of the process points towards this completion by the future of the individual being left open, even though that individual is confronted with God's promise because of the proximity of the kingdom of God in Jesus Christ and this promise transcends the ambivalence of the situation of freedom.

This irreversibility of salvation in history as the climax of that history is not automatically the salvation of the individual. It has to be freely accepted in faith, hope, and love as an offer of salvation. Rahner has said that God's irrevocable promise of himself which appeared in history must be its own reality in its state as a creature and not simply and solely in its divine origin. It is only when this event is in fact its own history, a historical reality which definitively determines man—in divine and, of course, also in creatural freedom—

and therefore becomes irrevocable, that we can speak, Rahner believes, of an absolute and 'eschatological' event of salvation. It is, in other words, only when the history of a man is really also the history of God himself that transcendence is definitively, absolutely and irreversibly present in history. It is only then that God's will to save becomes so effective in history that it can be said to be definitively present in it.

I now come to the fourth and last point—Rahner's insistence that the absolute bringer of salvation is in fact the irreversible event of salvation. Rahner has often pointed out, in the course of his career as a theologian, that Jesus Christ is the end of revelation, not because God arbitrarily set an end point, but because, although he in fact might have said much more, everything had been said in Jesus Christ. He therefore calls Jesus God's expression of himself in the strictest sense of the word. There is no more to be said.[58] Jesus, he declared recently, is the historical present of the last word of God's revelation of himself. Jesus himself claimed to be this and this claim was confirmed by his resurrection and made eternally valid. In this sense, then, he is the absolute bringer of salvation.

An Important Intermediate Consideration

If we are to understand Rahner's Christology properly, we must consider at this point an important intermediate question: Now that his aim is to some extent at least clear, what does Rahner really want to achieve in his transcendental Christology? Is it really more intelligible than the earlier Christology of the Church? Does it make it easier for modern man to believe in Jesus Christ? Does he not simply use different words which, in the last resort, are just as difficult to understand as the words of the Chalcedonian definition? To answer these closely related questions, we must first look back at what we have already said.

The aim of a transcendental Christology is to make the incarnation intelligible not on the basis of mythological ideas—for example, that God assumed human nature through which he acted simply as though he was hiding behind a mask—but rather from the point of view of man himself. Man wants to know explicitly, with a transcendental necessity of which he may not be explicitly conscious, the concrete promise made by God in history for which he has always hoped and of which he may have had no more than a presentiment. This promise made by God in history—it has to be made in history if the latter is to continue—must bring salvation to all men. This means that it must also be the definitive and irreversible promise of God himself. In addition to this, Rahner's 'Christology from below' has the advantage of offering man, on the basis of his own transcendental experiences, a certain help. It can help him to understand how God was able really to become man. He could do this because, in the incarnation, man's openness can be seen as an openness to God. Man cannot deduce this from his transcendental experiences because he does not know precisely how God is related to him in freedom, in other words, whether God is remote and rejecting or whether he is close and loving.

I can now go on to discuss Rahner's arguments about the historical Jesus a little more. According to the minimal statements, Jesus had a certain understanding of himself in any case. A human claim, however, is of little help if it is not confirmed and, in the case of Jesus' claim, which was very specific, confirmed by God. This confirmation was provided in the resurrection. 'Resurrection' should be interpreted in this context in the light of the Jewish meaning of the word. At the time of Jesus, Jews believed that the corporeal resurrection of the dead was reserved for the day when the definitive kingdom of God would be established, that is, at the end of time. It must therefore have been clear to the disciples and all those who heard the testimony that they bore to the resurrection of Jesus that Jesus was really the prophet of the end of time, the Messiah, the last prophet and the bringer of salvation. The fact that he had risen in a corporeality that could not be described or imagined, but was really transfigured could only mean that the God in whose name Jesus had appeared and with whom he knew himself to be associated in a unique way had confirmed the work and the message of the historical Jesus.

The word 'resurrection' or 'raising from the dead' had a quite definite meaning that was understood by every Jew. Wolfhart Pannenberg has had this to say about it: 'The unity of word and event in the appearances of the risen Christ is important in our understanding of how the event of the resurrection could have formed a basis for faith. If the resurrection or the appearances of the risen Christ had simply been crude facts and had not had a very special meaning as events, the origin of faith could not be more easily understood in the light of the events. Every event, however, has its own meaning within the context of its own historical tradition. In the case of the event of Jesus, it points to the beginning of the end, the confirmation of Jesus by God himself and definitive proof of the divinity of the God of Israel as the one God of all men'.[59]

In other words, then, if we want to avoid imputing conscious deceit to the disciples, we are bound to assume that they would not have dared to use the word 'resurrection' if their Lord had not really risen, since this word would have given the wrong impression to those who heard it. It is clear from many statements that he has made about the resurrection of Jesus in various articles that this is also Rahner's view.

It is possible to say that Rahner believes exclusively in the 'objective' resurrection of the Lord and cannot accept that the subjective experience of the disciples can be interpreted in any other way than as Jesus' real, corporeally transfigured state of being with God. He himself has said that an analysis of the texts referring to the resurrection, beginning with the simple formula 'he has risen', which have the form of confessions of faith, and concluding with the texts that dramatize the experience of Easter by means of various theological devices shows clearly that the disciples were quite conscious of the way in which the Easter event was experienced. This experience came from outside, Rahner insists. It was not a purely interior experience and was therefore different from the well-known visionary experiences. It was closely related to the crucified Jesus as an individual with his own particular fate, with the result that this fate and not just an existing person to whom something had happened was experienced as valid. This valid experience is what is given only in faith and what also gives foundation to that faith.

Whatever interpretation may be placed on the secondary questions, the fact of an objective resurrection of the Lord cannot be disputed in Rahner's theology. Even more important, however, in my opinion is Rahner's conviction that Christ 'rose' into our own hope of resurrection, with the result that the transcendental experience of expectation that is present in man's being is the sphere of understanding within which a phenomenon such as the resurrection of Jesus can be expected and experienced. Here too, it is clearly Rahner's aim to demonstrate that the event of the resurrection should not simply be accepted as a fact to be believed. However important it may be, even the call to the Jewish community at the time of Jesus to understand the resurrection does not satisfy Rahner. His aim has always been to show that the resurrection is not so strange as it might seem at first sight even to us today, in the light of our own experience of expectation. It is not true to say, he has suggested, that we can never approach the matter ourselves in the present century. We can certainly have a spiritual experience of Jesus' resurrection, since we can recognize his matter as living and victorious. Rahner has no intention, in making this claim, of denying the validity of the apostolic witness to the resurrection or of what was said at the beginning of this section. Even if we assume that there is a transcendental hope of resurrection and that we are always bound to look for tangible categorial evidence of that hope, a categorial name can only be given to its object and foundation in the apostles' witness to the resurrection of Jesus.

We may summarize by saying that, in developing his transcendental Christology, Rahner has always been anxious to stress man's transcendental hope of resurrection which exists in the event of the Lord's resurrection consciously as a reality—or at least as a real possibility—and as a promise for all men. There must be something in all men, he has always insisted, which makes it possible for them to understand the resurrection as a fulfilment of their expectations and it is this that makes the resurrection existentially meaningful and a possible object of faith.

This leads directly on to the theme of our important intermediate consideration and the question that we asked at the beginning: Is it really easier for modern man to believe in Jesus Christ following the transcendental approach? For Rahner, man expects the promise of divine salvation in history and therefore in Jesus Christ and this expectation may be quite unreflecting. In order to achieve its aim, his transcendental Christology has also to show that man is always practising a 'seeking' Christology. Rahner says that Christology can make, as it were, three appeals to man's general understanding of his own existence, which is already in a sense Christian because of prevenient grace and is never sufficiently capable of reflection, but certainly open to receive an appeal. (It makes these appeals, he claims, in a continuation that is more reflected and more filled with the content of one aspect of Christology.) These three appeals are in accordance with each other in that man is always practising this 'seeking' Christology. What, then, are the three related appeals to which Rahner refers in this context?

The first is love of one's neighbour. This concept has to be seen in its widest perspective and not confined to the most narrow circle of our fellow men. In the world-wide sense, love of one's neighbour can include, without changing its meaning, such a concept as justice. We also have to consider in this context why there should be such a phenomenon as love of one's neighbour and how it is justified. Love in this sense confronts us, after all, with a dilemma. It is absolute, radical and unconditioned. It takes risks in being directed without reserve towards the other. On the other hand, it is also subject to frequent disappointment, since the other person is finite and unreliable and cannot in himself justify the total commitment of radical love, but can call for sacrifice, renunciation and self-abandonment on the part of the one who loves, with the result that the question inevitably arises as to whether it is worth my while to work for others to have a better situation. Schilson has pointed out that 'in his love of his neighbour, man therefore always looks for the one in whom the love of God and the love of man are united so that, in giving oneself to that person there is no loss, but only gain.'[60] We do not, in other words, look past our fellow man, but in him for the one who justifies real love of our neighbour, since, where there is faith in Christ in the expression of love for our neighbour, as Rahner has said in the theological meditation to which we referred at the beginning of this chapter, 'there is also consent to him as the ground of that love. Either seeking or explicitly finding, this radical trust also loves, in man, a man (if it aims to be both absolute and human love at the same time), who is able to accept the radical nature of that love, support it and justify it with regard to man, without letting it become an adventure that destroys himself and others.'

The second phenomenon is one from which no man can escape and which also finds its answer in a transcendental Christology. This is the phenomenon of death, which Rahner calls the one fact which runs through and overshadows the whole of man's life. On the one hand, man must, in his freedom, take up an attitude towards death (as though he had to die many deaths in his life), although death, on the other hand, reveals the impotence of man and must therefore simply be endured. Is death therefore an acceptance of the absurdity of life which must be rejected under protest? Or is it just an appearance of meaninglessness and absurdity? Or can man also consent to death? As Schilson has observed, 'man can never give himself that certainty. It has rather to come up to him by a dying that does not remain in death, but rises again into the eternity of God and so overcomes the terror of death. In this way, Jesus Christ goes in search of enlightenment in the darkest moment of man's existence ahead of man and reconciles him by his own dying and rising again with the reversion to death of his being there'.[61]

(In this context, it is worth mentioning, parenthetically, two supplementary aspects of this phenomenon, although they do not occur in Rahner's discussion of the problem. In the first place, we would simply express a current attitude and say that no one has ever come back 'from above' or 'from heaven', even though we ought to know better as Christians. Secondly, we would also say that what man must accept, in his impotence and also in his freedom, and what he must 'cope' with is not so much death as a chance existence as such. An appeal to a 'seeking' Christology must take this fact into account and demonstrate that there is also an answer to this question in Christ.)

We have considered the first aspect, love, and the second, death. The third is hope. Man hopes and, planning and at the same time placing himself at the mercy of what cannot be predicted, goes towards his future, Rahner has said. His going towards the future is part of a constant attempt to diminish his inward and outward alienations from himself and to reduce the distance between what he is and what he wants and ought to be. This hope is also what keeps human history in motion. The clear and indisputable motivating force of all ideologies and of all human endeavour is that things may improve. The question, however, is: Is man's future—and therefore is man's hope—always exclusively directed towards something relatively better? Is the end always still to be reached in the future? Or does history bear its end (both individually and collectively) in itself? Does it in this sense, although it is still following its course, move already *in* its end? Man, who really hopes, must hope that these questions will be answered in the sense of the second of these alternatives by the reality of history itself. In the light of this hope, the Christian has an understanding, Rahner insists, of what is confessed by faith in the incarnation and resurrection of Jesus Christ as the irreversible beginning of the coming of God as the absolute future of the world and human history.

Salvation as Redemption

Let us now turn our attention to the soteriological aspect of Rahner's Christology. We are redeemed and saved in and through Christ. We have our salvation *in* him, but the question arises as to *through what* we are redeemed. What is the part played in this saving event by the cross of Jesus as the expiatory death for our sins?

In the first place, the cross of Jesus is not seen in isolation by Rahner. He always sees it in unity with the resurrection.

The death and resurrection of Jesus can only be understood, he has pointed out, if the inner relationship of unity existing between these two realities is clearly envisaged. Insofar as we can think meaningfully of a distance in time between the two events within the timeless context of the datum present in the resurrection, a temporal distance cannot be denied. The death of Jesus is a death that of its very nature was raised to a higher level in the resurrection. It was a dying into the resurrection, Rahner believes, and the resurrection was not the beginning of a new period in the life of Jesus which was filled with something new and different that continued time, but a continuation of the same, unique and unrepeatable life, now made definitive, as Jesus made his life definitive and lasting by his free death in obedience. If Jesus' fate has any soteriological significance at all, then that significance cannot, Rahner maintains, be found either in Jesus' death or in his resurrection individually, but can only be understood in the light of both aspects of the one event. Against this background, it is possible to ask whether any special redemptive function can be attributed to Jesus' crucifixion as such and in what sense it may be the cause of man's salvation.

Rahner rejects the theory of satisfaction which has been current in Catholicism since the Middle Ages and according to which God forgives men's sins only by means of the infinite satisfaction of the God-man on the cross, because sin is, in his view, an infinite offence against God. What is, however, surprising, at least at first sight, is that Rahner has not been able to derive much help from the New Testament concept of a sacrifice made by God of his blood shed for 'many'. This, he says, is for two reasons. On the one hand, he readily concedes that there are statements in the New Testament that can help us to understand the saving significance of the death of Jesus, because the idea of God's reconciliation with man by means of a sacrifice was widely accepted in Jewish society at that time as valid. On the other hand, however, we are bound to recognize two other factors. Firstly, the idea of sacrifice can help modern man very little to understand the soteriological aspect of Jesus' crucifixion. Secondly, there is no automatic connection between the idea of Jesus' death as a sacrifice bringing about reconciliation and the fundamental experience of Jesus both before and after the resurrection and indeed the whole Easter event.

If we want to do justice to Rahner's teaching about the redemption, we must not place the specific mode of Jesus' death, his death on the cross, in the centre of the soteriological event, but Jesus' obedient acceptance of death, which began with the incarnation itself. It is not surprising, then, that Rahner should find himself in sympathy with the physical doctrine of redemption found in some of the Greek Fathers of the Church and say that, according to this teaching, the world is saved simply because it is physically indissolubly linked, in the humanity of Jesus, with God. This sympathy with the physical redemption of the world can be found in many of Rahner's writings and especially those in which he speaks about the reconciliation between God and man brought about by the incarnation.

Rahner insists, then, that Jesus handed himself over totally to the Father in his death. He trusted the Father completely in death. He had no more security and could not assert his claim in death. He was able only to accept his death obediently in the hope that his claim would be received and confirmed by God. I am of the opinion—and I may be going further here than Rahner himself would go—that Jesus' contingent death on the cross as his crucifixion only has a saving significance insofar as the whole of humanity in its complete impotence appears in Jesus. The scandal of the cross was, for Jesus' disciples, precisely this disillusionment, namely that a Messiah could not and ought not to die in precisely that way. Walter Kasper has commented in this context: 'The impotence, poverty and insignificance with which the kingdom of God dawned in the person and the work of Jesus Christ were finally confirmed in the scandal of the cross. Jesus' life ended in a final openness. His history and his fate remain a question to which only God can give an answer. If Jesus' appearance is not to be a total failure, the only possible answer is that the new era dawned with his death. But this is, of course, the content of the confession of Jesus' resurrection'.[62]

We can see therefore that, according to Rahner, Jesus' crucifixion brings about man's salvation because the climax of human impotence is combined in it with the absolute trust in the Father. Whether or not this might have been manifested in a different death or if Jesus had died differently must remain a matter for purely theoretical speculation. We are saved and redeemed because Jesus and in him God himself accepted this ultimate impotence of death—a powerlessness that can only either be accepted in trust or rejected in despair—and because this acceptance began with the incarnation and was made definitive in death. We can therefore understand, in the light of this teaching, what Rahner means by 'soteriology'. He has in fact said that a soteriology that only points, in Jesus' death, to a contingent or chance mode of satisfaction that might have been achieved in a different way, that is, by something other than death, is a distortion of the central significance of Jesus' death. It can therefore never succeed in making intelligible the inner redemptive significance of our dying in Christ as the radical and definitive event of subjective redemption.

In our understanding of Rahner's soteriology (as a doctrine of redemption), it is very important to remember that here, as in other aspects of his theology, Rahner does not see redemption as functioning mythologically, as though God had somehow to be made to change his mind by Jesus' crucifixion and so led to save men in this way. God's will to save, Rahner has always taught, is stronger than human sin and cannot be frustrated by human sin. It is always present, no matter what happens in human history.

Rahner's three appeals, to love of one's neighbour, death, and hope, with which he turns to modern man and in which it is relatively unimportant whether they are complete in themselves or are extended to cover other aspects of human experience,[63] point clearly to sin as a guilty incapacity to transcend oneself and lose oneself in God. On the one hand, these appeals point to what redemption from guilt can mean today. On the other hand, they are also an appeal to that aspect of humanity that man is seeking, to what he is able to be if he hands himself over in faith, hope, and love to Jesus the Christ and then ceases to live simply as a man and begins to live as someone who is drawn into Christ and really participates in his life, death, and resurrection. Such a man is not simply imitating Christ. He is supernaturally participating in accordance with his being and this participation is, Rahner thinks, the result of the eternal significance of the humanity of Jesus for our relationship with God. We are redeemed and saved because, in the strength and grace of Christ and by virtue of his mediation, we are able to do what is of fundamental importance—we are able to respond to the three appeals and love our neighbour, accept death, and continue to hope.

If it is seen in this light, redemption ceases to appear as a one-sided reality that is restricted to man in his guilt. If we think of it in this way, we can experience it actively because it points to the one who makes it possible for us to believe, hope, and love. In this way too, it is also the answer to the question: *Cur Deus homo?*—Why did God become man. It would in any case seem that redemption and salvation are only possible because what could not simply be decreed by God has taken place in Jesus Christ—man's deification in him. As Rahner says, the resurrection of Christ is, in its deepest being, and not simply because of a legal acceptance of God, the event in which God not only accepts his creature irrevocably as his own reality, but also transfigures that creature, deifying him to such an extent that this transfiguration occurs and continues as the creatures's total acceptance of his being divinely accepted in his freedom.

·7·

Faith and the Church

This introduction to Rahner's theological thought would not be complete without at least a short concluding chapter on his ecclesiology. My chief aim here will be to outline the distinguishing features and the specific approaches of his teaching about the Church, and of the relationship between the Church and faith in his writings.

Rahner calls the Church the 'primordial sacrament' and insists that he does not use the term as a vague adaptation of the basic concept of 'sacrament' as employed in the Church's normal sacramental theology. On the contrary, he claims to have derived the term from Christology. It points to the single, lasting, incarnate, and structured presence of eschatological salvation in Christ in the form of a sign, a presence in which the sign and the signified are 'without confusion and without division'. God's grace is present in the flesh, as it were, of a historical and ecclesiosological reality which cannot be emptied by what is signified because, if this were so, the grace of Christ, who continues to be man eternally, would be temporary and something that can be superseded, and because we would then be still in the Old Testament situation.

This understanding of the Church clearly distinguishes the Catholic Church from other possible understandings of the reality of the Church. The term 'sacrament' was used to describe the Church in the Second Vatican Council and this indicates that the historical and eschatological promise of salvation given by God in Jesus Christ does not simply continue to exist in the inner life and subjective faith of Christians, but that grace cannot lose its incarnate structure and that there are, within the Church, places in which the grace of Christ is perpetuated, whatever the situation may be with regard to the sinfulness, either individually or collectively, in the Church at any given time.

At the same time, however, the term 'sacrament' as applied to the Church does not necessarily have to be seen as dividing the churches, even though it distinguishes the Catholic Church's understanding of itself. This is because the answer that all Christians would give to the question: **How have men received the fulness of God's revelation through the centuries in a way that it has continued to be the real word of God and not simply the word of men?** would be: Through the tradition of the Church.

Jesus' disciples experienced the event of Jesus of Nazareth, his life, teaching, death, and resurrection as the event that would bring about God's salvation in them, and they knew at the same time that it was the definitive promise of salvation made to the whole of mankind. That is why they bore witness to the Lord. This apostolic witness formed the lasting foundation of the whole Christian tradition. It is, however, clearly not the function of this witness to enable a past event to remain in men's memories as a subjective idea. To go beyond this, it is important for man to be able to encounter Christ himself within the tradition of the Church and in the Church itself. Christ is, after all, the only mediator of salvation and the Church is that mediator only in a derived sense—Christ brings about salvation in and through the Church.

One of the greatest achievements of Vatican II was to set the Catholic concept of tradition free from the narrow confines within which it had become trapped in the period

following the Council of Trent. According to the Dogmatic
Constitution on Divine Revelation, tradition is not primarily
a content handed down in statements and practices which
always remains the same, but the lived faith of the people of
God, since the Church 'in her teaching, life, and worship
perpetuates and hands on to all generations all that she
herself is and all that she believes'.[64] Tradition, then, is not a
previously given, objective factor. It is not Holy Scripture,
nor the handing down of truths and pious forms that have
not been written down in Scripture, nor even the adminis-
tration of the sacraments. It is primarily the lived faith of the
Church. Even before the Second Vatican Council, a fundamental structure of Rahner's ecclesiology can be derived
from this, since it is obvious to Rahner that the Church's
expression of faith should ultimately be the norm of faith
and of all criticism of tradition. In his theology in general,
man's expression of life and faith takes precedence over
reflection.

Scripture as the Constant Norm of Faith

This fundamental structure of Rahner's ecclesiology has
had a clear effect on his attitude towards Scripture as the
constant norm of faith in the particular case of the formation of the canon of Scripture. It is interesting in this context
to compare Protestant and Catholic attitudes. According to
Martin Luther, on the one hand, the canon of Scripture has
a binding force on the individual believer. On the other
hand, the Catholic Church has always appealed to oral
tradition. Rahner does neither one nor the other, and
believes that the decision as to what belongs to the canon of
Scripture and what does not can only be made by the lived
faith of the Church, to which we have referred above as the
ultimate criterion of tradition in Rahner's view. The faith
and life of the early Church were made objective in written

documents and this objectivization is still regarded as successful. It has indeed always been accepted and has therefore become the norm in the Church. Hence it is not an insuperable difficulty that the formation of the canon of Scripture and the recognition of its representative aspect as an objectivization of the apostolic Church should not simply coincide in time, since it is well-known that the canon was not formed until after the end of the apostolic era.

The same applies to the inspiration of Scripture and its inerrancy, two subjects that are closely related to each other. It has been stated in papal encyclicals from the time of Leo XIII until the pontificate of Pius XII that God does not have to be used in psychological theories as the literary *auctor* of Scripture; as Rahner has pointed out, the foundation of the Church by God himself through the Spirit in Jesus Christ, the establishment of the apostolic Church as the norm for the Church of the future, and the acceptance of Scripture as a constitutive element of the early Church are all sufficient evidence, both in the positive and in the restricting sense, that God is the author of Scripture and that he inspired it. There is, therefore, Rahner concludes, no need for any special theory of psychological inspiration in this case. If God wanted the Church, then he obviously also wanted Scripture, because it was necessary for Scripture to develop in the Church as the norm for all times. The result of this, according to Rahner, is that the human authors of Scripture worked in exactly the same way as all other human authors and they had no need to know anything consciously about the fact that they were inspired.

The same can be said of the inerrancy of Scripture. Rahner is of the opinion that the only statements that are free of error in Scripture are those which God wanted to record especially for the sake of our salvation, although he recognizes the existence of problems connected with this statement and left unsolved by Vatican II. These problems have arisen from the fact that historical statements are inevitably made in connection with a historical event and these may be faithful records of the event insofar as they are in accordance with the author's intention. They have also occurred as a result of the Church's tradition. Rahner has commented that, in the past, the inerrancy of Scripture was undoubtedly interpreted in too narrow a sense. It was often understood in the sense of a verbal inspiration, and the sacred writers were regarded as God's secretaries and not as independent authors writing in a historically conditioned way. However interesting these problems and their causes are, I cannot unfortunately go into them here. All that I can do in this context is to point to the fundamental structure of Rahner's theology—that is, the incarnate structure of grace—and note that it has led to results which, although we accept them now without question, caused considerable difficulties in the field of theology until as late as the nineteen-fifties.

Rahner's approach to ecclesiology has borne fruit in his sacramental theology. He has dealt with the sacraments from the historical and from the pastoral theological points of view. The progress that he has made in renewing the approach to the sacraments can only be measured with reasonable accuracy by those who have studied the Church's traditional sacramental theology at some depth. The most obvious consequence of his ecclesiological approach, in which the Church is seen as the primordial sacrament, is what might reasonably be called the sacramental structure of the whole reality of faith. When we receive the sacraments, Rahner believes, we are not simply people who have something to do with God, who are receiving grace and in whom an event is taking place—God's communication with us. The history of salvation takes place and God reveals himself to man every time he opens himself to the incomprehensible mystery of God and allows himself to enter that

mystery, and every time he accepts his supernatural transcendentality in intercommunication with God and in love
and faithfulness, and commits himself to a task in the world
that is open to the future. What we call the Church, Rahner
says, and defines the Church as the explicit and official
history of salvation, and what we call the sacraments are
fundamentally only especially concrete and historically
tangible events in that wider history of salvation that is
identical with man's life as a whole.

It is clear, then, that, faithful to his original anthropological approach, Rahner tries to see the Church as the
primordial sacrament and the individual sacraments as
expressions of the life of the Church and has tried at the
same time to develop this vision in the light of a more
universal understanding. The sacraments are therefore
'only' the climax of what man does as a man and a believer.
This does not mean that Rahner wants to level down or do
away with the distinction between the Christian's explicit
expression of his faith in receiving the sacraments and his
everyday life. The sacraments are, after all, something that
everyday life can never be. Each sacrament is the visible,
tangible place of the eschatologically valid activity of the
Lord in his community. It is the presence of Christ in the
form of an explicit sign and the lasting guarantee of his
saving power that does not depend on the person adminis-
tering the sacrament.

This, of course, is what is known in the traditional
theology of the Church as the *opus operatum* of the sacraments. Rahner is convinced that the sacraments are only
effective in faith, hope and love. They have nothing to do
with magic and do not compel God in any way. They are
actions performed by God, who is free, with us, who are also
free. They are only effective insofar as we are free and open
to them.

However important a part this may play in Rahner's teaching—and however difficult it may be to put the stress marks in the right places—it is, in my opinion, even more important to point out in this context that Rahner regards the sacraments as expressions of the life of the Church, or as the Church's way of making itself present in the lives of individual believers. This particular emphasis has made it possible for him to dispense with any explicit attempt to establish the institution of each individual sacrament by Jesus Christ himself. From the very beginning of the Church as the primordial sacrament, it has always been possible to see—and this is also of importance if our dogmatic arguments in the case of the institution of all the sacraments by Christ are to be effective—that the existence of real sacraments in the most traditional sense is not necessary and has in any case to be founded on a particular word, either factual or presumed, in which the historical Jesus speaks explicitly of a particular sacrament. A real act on the part of the Church, forming part of the essence of the Church as the historical and eschatological saving presence directed towards the individual in his own special situation, is in itself a sacrament even if reflection about this sacramental characteristic, which flows from the essence of the Church, does not follow until much later. Rahner's reasoning here is clearly not a traditional argument tracing the sacraments laboriously back to the presumably explicit will of Christ. (In any case, Rahner himself believes that this traditional argument is only unambiguous in the case of the Eucharist.) It is quite clear from Rahner's argument as outlined in this paragraph that the fact of the sacraments emerges from the being of the Church itself. One could almost say, with a rather crude simplification, that if there were no sacraments, the Church would have to introduce them.

What part do the sacraments play in the existential

experience of individual Christians? In the first place, Rahner stresses that the individual is always oriented towards the community, with the result that individual salvation as such is not possible. Secondly, however, the individual is always, in existentially significant situations in his life, incorporated through the sacraments into the death and resurrection of the Lord and consequently into the Christian community. The individual sacraments should, on the one hand, be seen in the light of the Church as the fundamental and primordial sacrament and, on the other, be fitted into the history of the individual, since they act, at existentially significant moments in the life of the individual Christian as the visible sacramental appearance of the Christian life of grace. These individual sacraments are, of course, the sacraments of initiation (baptism and confirmation), the sacraments conferring status (marriage and ordination), the sacraments of forgiveness (penance and the anointing of the sick), and especially the Eucharist, which is perhaps the sacrament of sacraments.

Rahner's fundamental approach can be traced in all the aspects of his ecclesiology that I have considered in this chapter. The lived faith of the Church, which is, of course, the lived faith of all believers, enables the Church to be as it is, despite the presence of sin in the Church and because of the help of the Spirit of Christ. There is, apart from the Church, no authority that is qualified to decide about the canon of Scripture or the inerrancy or inspiration of that Scripture. Again, apart from the Church, there is also no authority that can determine the number or the effects of the sacraments. And all this is derived from the one fact that the Church is the primordial sacrament in which Christ lives on and in which there are, on the basis of the incarnate structure of grace, places where man is able, despite his weakness and guilt, to encounter Christ.

The Question of the True Church

The Church as a whole is the norm of faith and of the criticism of tradition. In the context of this statement, something has to be said in this chapter about the vexed question of the true Church. As far as it is possible for me to judge, Rahner has never been a leading theologian of the ecumenical movement, although it cannot be denied that, both in his personal contacts and in his theology, he has done a great deal to build bridges between the Catholic Church and the non-Catholic churches. He is also perhaps even more aware than most other theologians of the aspects that separate the churches, but this does not prevent him from seeing, beyond what separates, the many more unifying factors and from acknowledging that Protestant Christianity has a very positive contribution to make to Catholic faith.

On the other hand, however, Rahner's whole theological background gives him every reason not to remain silent about what separates Christians and about the question of the true Church, even though he believes firmly in the possibility of salvation for all men and all the more firmly in the possibility that all Christians will be saved. In view of this total vision, it is not surprising that he should depart from the ways of traditional fundamental theology and postulate an indirect method of justifying the Catholic Church as the Church of Christ. He declared recently that, according to the traditional method of fundamental theology, direct historical proof is furnished to show that the Roman Catholic Church is the Church of Christ and that Christ wanted that Church to be as it is in its essential structure and in accordance with its own understanding of itself, as deriving from Christ in direct historical continuity. Rahner does not think that this interpretation is fundamentally impossible, but he does believe that it is extremely difficult for a contemporary Christian, living at a distance of two thousand years from Christ, to accept. It would, in other words, call for such a number of difficult historical proofs that it is in practice at least impossible for the ordinary Catholic to grasp, given the possibilities of knowledge and truth available to him now.

Rahner's solution to this problem is perhaps surprising. According to him, every Christian, whatever his confession may be, has the right to presume that his own historically developed confession is the legitimate one for him, since even a Catholic cannot act differently. In order to avoid ecclesiological relativism—and this is, in the opinion of Rahner, who is moreover firmly opposed to it, quite widespread today—he has suggested certain criteria which can be applied to the true Church, even though it is impossible to establish their historical validity.

The first of these criteria is that the Christian should ask himself where the Church of Christ is to be found—the Church with the densest, simplest and most tangible continuity with early Christianity. The second criterion is the safeguarding of the fundamental substance of Christianity and the third is the question of objective authority. No prior judgment is made by these formal criteria, but, as Rahner points out, it is possible that a Protestant theologian may agree with them, but would perhaps find the objectivity of the Church in the objectivity of the written word of God in the New Testament. In other words, controversial theology could begin with the need to test these formal criteria against the concrete form of the churches. Of the three fundamental principles of Reformation Christianity—*sola gratia, sola fide, sola scriptura,* the sole validity of grace, faith and Scripture—perhaps it is only the last, Scripture, that is really controversial and therefore really divisive, with the result that it may be the root of all the other factors that divide the churches.

As we pointed out above, according to all the Christian churches, the Church is founded on tradition and has been promised the help of the Holy Spirit. On the one hand, the tradition of the Church is certainly more than the written, reflected and objectively recorded documents. On the other, Christian faith must also be defined with regard to other religions. Indeed, we may go further and say that it must be continuously brought up to date in confrontation with the problems of the modern world. This leads to the obviously important problem that there must also be a post-biblical tradition and this tradition may also become the norm of the Church. According to Protestant theologians, all post-biblical tradition must always remain open to possible re-examination and the only valid criterion for the tradition of the Church and the criticism of tradition is Scripture. Is this perhaps true? The Reformers demanded, consistently for a historical religion in which many abuses had taken root, a return to the sources—Scripture—so that the ballast that had accumulated in the course of centuries of Christian faith could be thrown away. Rahner's views on this question are of some interest here.

It is quite understandable that the Catholic Church should have taken over the point of departure of Protestant Christianity and tried to trace tradition back to the apostolic era. This attempt was made after the Reformation at the Council of Trent, not very successfully, it has to be admitted, in the case of Scripture, and more convincingly by developing the idea of a 'second source' of revelation, the oral tradition coming from the apostles. The New Testament writings can be regarded as a body of work written by different authors which came together more or less by chance and which cannot claim to represent the whole of the content of faith that was present in the early Church. If this is the case, it can be reasonably assumed that the faith of the early Church was wider in many respects than it would appear to be from the record in the New Testament scriptures. There would therefore not appear to be any compelling reason for assuming that the New Testament is the only lasting norm of faith for all time in the later Church, because it does not contain the whole essential deposit of faith of Christianity. It is moreover difficult for us today, with our historical consciousness, to believe that such contents of faith, not recorded in Scripture, could have survived throughout the centuries without any change or adulteration as cultures and languages changed. It would be wrong to appeal here to the Holy Spirit, or even to what the Church has 'always believed and taught', in the second case certainly because it could hardly be justified from the point of view of the history of dogma.

There is another question that theologians of the Reformed tradition have to ask their Catholic colleagues. On the one hand, it is difficult to understand that there should be no attempt to bring traditional teaching up to date or to define it against errors that cannot later be nullified. (Examples of this are the first Councils which dealt with Christology and the Trinity.) On the other hand, it is not quite clear to Protestants why, in the case of dogmas such as the Marian dogmas and the dogma of papal infallibility that have been defined since the Reformation, attempts should have been made to establish that Scripture has in fact been applied to a contemporary situation and that such attempts are valid and justified, on the basis of Scripture itself, for all periods of history. The question therefore arises for Catholic theolgians—who must apparently deny it *a priori*—as to whether in such cases something new is not being defined as divine revelation which is, in fact, no more than a pious conviction that has made its appearance since the end of the apostolic era.

The Catholic answer to this question would be that dogmatic statements are obligatory only when truths revealed by God for our salvation are involved. If the whole of the Church's ministry of the word, including that carried out by the teaching office of the Church, is carried subject to Scripture and the books of Scripture teach 'firmly, faithfully, and without error that truth which God wanted to put into the sacred writings for the sake of our salvation',[65] then this must also apply to the infallible statements that have been made in the post-apostolic tradition of the Church. These pronouncements must also be verified, as historical expressions of faith, for their value in connection with the salvation of men living at the period. It is only if this is done that any attempt can be made to transfer those contents of faith that have been given expression in the Church's tradition to the framework of contemporary thought and language. These contents can only be falsified if pronouncements made in the past by the Church's teaching office are transplanted as they are, without reflection, into the present. It is also worth remembering in this context that the term that Rahner uses so frequently—a 'hierarchy of values'—was originally coined by the Second Vatican Council.

What does this expression mean? It does not mean that the Catholic can reject a statement that has been made about faith during the history of the Church and that has been defined by the Church as a dogma. It does mean, however, that he can confess with an easy conscience that a dogma that has been defined by the Church's magisterium at a given period, in a particular form of words and in a certain situation, may be too far removed from the central message of Christianity for it to have any real meaning for him in his practical and religious life. The Catholic Christian is able, in other words, to leave a great deal to his implicit faith, while consenting to the lasting truth of defined contents of faith.

It is almost taken for granted in Catholic theology that not everything that has been revealed forms a necessary part of the Christian's knowledge of faith and that the truth of a dogmatic statement, for example, is not dependent on whether the individual Christian recognizes it or does not recognize it as a making present of Scripture and Christian faith that is of importance in his own life. As Rahner's term 'hierarchy of truths' suggests, this applies even more to those doctrines that do not refer so directly or so recognizably nowadays to God's act of salvation brought about in Christ. (Examples of such doctrines are clearly those relating to Mary.) This may, of course, be simply because a twentieth-century Christian no longer clearly understands the aspect of salvation that is contained in these dogmas.

Bearing these conditions in mind, it is still very difficult to see why there should not be, subject to the help of the Holy Spirit to which Scripture bears clear witness, a growth in the entire Church's understanding of tradition.[66] If tradition were understood in this way, the Church as a whole (and it is the Church as a whole which is infallible) might recognize a given insight into faith as binding for all time and not simply for the time when it was made explicit.

It is not true to say that a recognition of tradition of this kind would expose the word of God to the arbitrary decision of a human teaching office or a human pope, since only what has been believed for a long time in the Church and is known to belong to the substance of faith can be defined as dogma. Not only have there never been any official definitions of faith resulting from the piety of a pope or a minority in the Church—such definitions simply could not occur. The opposite is also true—it is equally impossible for the Christological statements made by the first Councils of the Church (which are, as such, not contained in Scripture and whose opponents could also appeal to Scripture!) to be denied by an individual Christian or for slavery (which was obviously tolerated at the time of the New Testament) ever again to be acceptable to Christian teaching.

It should not be forgotten—and this also applies to Protestantism—that faith in Jesus of Nazareth is not given to man in the form of the dead letter of Scripture alone. It is above all a living faith, existing in the confession of those who believe. This is the way in which God offers his grace to men—as Rahner would say, he offers it to them 'categorially'. If this is borne in mind, our trust in the help of the Holy Spirit that was promised to the Christian community by the Lord himself will be justified in ultimate decisions and pronouncements about faith. It will be recognized that it is quite possible for a lived faith to be made present and articulated in such a way that this articulation is permanently known as revealed in Jesus Christ, even if a contemporary Christian's insight into a particular apsect of faith is not equal to the insight that existed in the past.

A Catholic Christian knows that his faith in the Church's tradition is not exposed either to the arbitrary decision of a human teaching office or to whatever happens to be the prevailing exegetical fashion at the moment. He is also not at the mercy of his own subjective insights. Above all, he knows that his own faith would suffer if a proposition that had once been defined by the whole Church as belonging to the substance of faith could at any time be declared as false and thus made null and void.

The Development of Dogma and the Right of the Individual in the Church

In the preceding section, I discussed Rahner's contribution to the controversial question of the true Church, but I have not dealt with the important and very difficult problems of the criticism of the specifically Catholic tradition, the bringing up to date of faith, and the relationship between the individual Christian and the Church's teaching office. I shall examine these problems in the light of Rahner's teaching in this final section.

Rahner has often concerned himself with the question of the development of dogma and the interpretation of dogma and in this question has made it clear that he does not share Hans Küng's opinion that the fulfilment of purely formal conditions does not guarantee the truth of all the defined statements made by the Church's teaching office. Unlike Küng, he believes that all real dogmas are infallibly true statements and thinks that the rules of biblical hermeneutics should be applied to the interpretation of the pronouncements made by the Church's teaching office. These rules have gradually come to be applied to biblical exegesis in the Catholic Church since the Enlightenment and they have, after a long and difficult period of development, also come to be explicitly or implicitly recognized by the Church's *magisterium*. They must also, Rahner inisists, so long as the changes that are necessary for their adaptation to the new task are made, be regarded as rules to be used in interpreting the later dogmas of the Church. It is important to bear in mind here, Rahner has pointed out, that dogmatic truths of an obligatory kind can also be expressed and handed down together with or in the form of models containing other non-dogmatic and therefore non-obligatory ideas. These other ideas are passed on automatically with the dogmatic pronouncements and can later be shown to be non-obligatory and even as false statements.

There is therefore a clear task confronting dogmatic theologians today—to provide an orthodox interpretation of the Church's dogmas. It is, up to now, a task that has only been carried out here and there and is in no sense complete. It has nonetheless already been clearly demonstrated, by

Rahner among others, that it would be quite wrong to accept
the existing truths of faith, even when they have been
defined by the Church's teaching office, just as they are, in
the form in which they have been expressed. Words, after
all, change their meaning in the course of history. Even
more important is the fact that ways of thinking also change
from generation to generation, with the result that a literal
handing down and rendering of pronouncements made by
the Church's teaching office should also be a translation into
the present, since the difference between the way of
thinking in which the statement was originally made and the
contemporary way of thinking cannot be eliminated and
modern man, especially if he is not skilled in history, will
automatically interpret the faith of past centuries in a way
that is different from the original intention. Finally, as
Rahner has pointed out, a great deal is contained and
presupposed, often implicitly, in an earlier mode of thinking or form of expression that has no meaning for later
generations or is even regarded as false by them. We may
summarize this by saying that it is as difficult to understand a
dogma as it is to understand the real meaning of Scripture.

It should therefore be clear that it cannot, as was
apparently the case in earlier, traditional theology, be the
primary task of theology and the Church's teaching office
simply to repeat what has already been said and defend it.
The dogmas of the Church, which are not and cannot be a
making present of Scripture as the lasting norm of the
Church, should not have the importance that many
theologians—and especially Roman theologians—have
tended to give them. Rahner has made this clear on several
occasions. He has stressed, for example, that the teaching
office ought not to have the task of defining so-called new
dogmas on the one hand and anxiously safeguarding the
purity of already defined dogmas on the other. It should
rather be concerned with preserving the whole faith of the

Church in its fundamental substance, not so much by exercising a strict censorship as by positively encouraging collaboration in the task of re-interpreting faith in a new and changing environment which cannot be assumed to be Christian. The personal and material resources at the disposal of the Roman authorities would be subjected to considerable strain by a new task of this kind, and the *magisterium* has for many years to a great extent continued to work in the old way and with the same resources. If it is to safeguard its independent status and continue to perform its special function in the Church, while at the same time maintaining the confidence of Christians acting correctly and efficiently in accordance with people's consciousness of faith, it must, Rahner insists, find a new creative style in teaching and exercising discipline. I do not think that I would be misinterpreting Rahner if I were to say that he is of the opinion that the real task of the Church's teaching office today is to place less emphasis on already defined dogmas, and to re-interpret the fundamental substance of faith, both by making it possible for this task to be carried out by the Church as a whole and by contributing actively to it itself.

Rahner has always insisted that by no means all the pronouncements made by the Church's teaching office are infallible dogmas in the strict sense of the word, and that it would be true to say that only relatively few of these pronouncements are infallible in this sense. The question therefore arises: What should the Christian's attitude towards such statements be, in view of the fact that they are invested with the authority of the teaching office, but may even be false? In practice, Rahner has observed, authentic statements and teachings issued by the Church's teaching office which can be changed (and may therefore be erroneous) are treated as though they were realities that had to be respected for ever. Even Vatican II did not provide a solution to this problem, since, as Rahner indicated, there was no clear insight into how recognition of the supreme teaching authority of the Church and the sincere loyalty that is required in connection with the purely authentic teachings that emanate from Rome might exist side by side with a critical attitude towards those teachings, a criticism which may even be a right and a duty on the part of professional theologians.

Rahner's repeated criticism of the Church's teaching authority is that its members lack the strength of will to admit when they have made erroneous decisions and the honesty to state that such pronouncements are wrong when they have been proved to be wrong. This is all the more tragic in the case of papal encyclicals such as *Humanae Vitae* on the use of contraceptives and other official documents dealing with such matters as the possibility of ordaining women as priests. These publications have a direct bearing on the practical life of the Catholic Christian and therefore lead to a crisis in the conscience of precisely those people who are predisposed to take the statements made by the Church seriously. In this sphere, Rahner has undoubtedly performed a very positive service.

As far as I can see, he was the first to outline norms of behaviour for the conscience of the individual Christian in connection with *Humanae Vitae*. These norms were taken over, at least in essence, by the Conference of German Bishops and published in 1967.[67] It is worth quoting from this document: 'The Church cannot always let itself be confronted, in its teaching and practice, with the choice of either making a binding decision regarding faith or simply remaining silent and leaving everything to the opinion of each individual. Anyone, however, who privately holds the opinion that he already has the Church's better future insight must question his conscience in God's presence, assessing his own attitude in sober self-criticism and trying to discover whether he has the necessary depth and breadth of specialized theological knowledge to deviate in his own private theory and practice from the present teaching of the Church. A case of this kind is quite conceivable'.[68]

There are few theologians in the Church who have so consistently championed the rights of the individual as Rahner. Two of the fundamental concepts of his ecclesiology are pluralism and toleration in the Church. This is very much in accordance with the central, constant theme in his theology. I have drawn attention again and again in this book to this scarlet thread running through his theology—his desire to translate faith into the present and in this way to make it intelligible to modern man from within, that is, from man's point of view. We are not required, out of respect for the Church's authority, to behave as though every theological view in the Church was simply an obedient repetition of a declaration by the teaching office, he has said. There is an open system in the Catholic Church in which the most widely differing factors—the instinct of believers, new knowledge on the part of the individual Christians and theologians, and new situations giving rise to new questions, to name only a few—all work together to clarify the Church's consciousness of faith.

Finally, from his own experience Rahner knows how it is always possible for conflicts to arise in the Church. He himself has been at the centre of fierce controversy, in spite of—or perhaps because of—his fundamental and passionate faithfulness to the Catholic Church. In the past, changes have been brought about in the Church, which does not simply accumulate rolls of fame in its annals, by charismatic Christians and this is likely to continue in the future. It is obvious that such Christians are bound to suffer from the Church as an institution and from its directives and disciplinary measures. What is important, however, is that it is still possible for members of the Church to suffer because of the Church. Rahner is one who suffers in this way.

Notes

1. H.-J. Fischer in the *Frankfurter Allgemeine Zeitung,* 29 October 1976.

2. H. Vorgrimler, *Karl Rahner. Leben—Denken—Werke* (Munich, 1963), p. 83. Cardinal Joseph Ratzinger has expressed a very similar opinion in his discussion of Rahner's *Grundkurs des Glaubens* (Eng. trans.; *Foundations of Christian Faith*) in the *Theologische Revue* 74 (1978), p. 186.

3. *Herder-Korrespondenz* 28 (1974), p. 79.

4. Similarly, I have not discussed the objections to Rahner's theology.

5. *Wagnis des Christen* (Freiburg, 1974), pp. 27–40 (Eng. trans.; *Christian at the Crossroads*).

6. See Rahner's *Schriften zur Theologie* XIII, pp. 11–47 (*Theological Investigations,* 13).

7. This idea has also appeared in the history of philosophy and especially in the work of Descartes.

8. This is a methodological process used in fundamental—not fringe—theological problems and is in no sense a questioning of faith.

9. *The Critique of Pure Reason,* B 25.

10. See, for example, J.B. Lotz, 'Zur Thomas-Rezeption in der Maréchal-Schule', *Theologie und Philosophie* 49 (1974), pp. 375–394 and *ibid., Transzendentale Erfahrung* (Freiburg, 1978).

11. See F. Ricken, 'Sind Sätze über Gott sinnlos? Theologie und Sprache in der analytischen Philosophie', K.-H. Weger, ed., *Religionskritik* (Munich, 1976), pp. 101–21.

12. This is why he often speaks about 'stammering' about God.

13. H.G. Gadamer, *Philosophische Hermeneutik* (Tübingen, 1967), p. 52.

14. The term *rudes* is a theological word for those who are theologically lay people.

15. L. Kolakowski, *Die Gegenwart des Mythos* (Munich, 1973).

16. *Op. cit.*, p. 47.

17. For transcendental experiences, see also below, the section entitled 'Transcendence as an Experience of Grace', pp. 89–95.

18. See K. Rahner and H. Vorgrimler, *Concise Theological Dictionary* (London, 1965), 'Proof of the Existence of God', pp. 381–83.

19. Or, to be more precise, he was too interested in the possibility of 'synthetic judgments *a priori*'.

20. This is what I have called the absence of content in transcendental experiences.

21. To prevent any misunderstanding from occurring: Being able to fly is not a condition for the possibility of my existence, so there is no need for any flying beings!

22. R. Garaudy, J.B. Metz and K. Rahner, *Der Dialog* (Reinbek, 1966), p. 87.

23. For the whole, see Neuner and Roos, *Der Glaube der Kirche in den Urkunden der Lehrverkündigung*, revised by K. Rahner and K.-H. Weger (Regensburg, 1975), No. 332.

24. See P. Overhage & K. Rahner, *Hominisation* (London, 1965), where the most thorough exposition and development of this idea of Rahner's will be found.

25. B. Weissmahr, *Gottes Wirken in der Welt* (Frankfurt, 1973), p. 130.

26. This 'entirely' applied to man and 'entirely' applied to God is a theological statement accepted by Rahner which only appears to be contradictory when the fundamentally different nature of God's activity is forgotten. The more man is active, the more God is active—the causes cannot be separated, even though they are situated at different levels.

27. H. Plessner, 'Der Mensch als Lebewesen', R. Ročeck and O. Schatz, eds., *Philosophische Anthropologie heute* (Munich, 1972), p. 63.

28. It is not difficult to show the influence of this theologoumenon of Rahner's on some of the statements in the documents of Vatican II.

29. 'Ontic' means 'in accordance with being', in other words, what is; 'ontological', in the sense in which Rahner uses the term, means becoming conscious of what is 'ontic'.

30. To avoid misunderstandings, it should be pointed out that Rahner's supernatural existential factor does not form the basis of Christian faith, but rather presupposes it. It provides an answer only to certain theologically pressing questions.

31. A study of the chronological development of Rahner's thought can be found in K. Lehmann and Karl Rahner, *Bilanz der Theologie im 20. Jahrhundert* (Freiburg, 1970), p. 170.

32. I would mention in this context Rahner's meditation *Everyday Faith*.

33. H. Denzinger and A. Schönmetzer, eds., *Enchiridion Symbolorum Definitionum et Declarationum* (Freiburg, 33 1965), 1351.

34. Neuner and Roos, *op. cit.*, No. 372–74.

35. Entelechy refers to man's innermost being, the factor that determines his action.

36. This 'formal object' is not the object contemplated, but the consideration under which an object or a sum total of objects is regarded.

37. The term *nouvelle théologie* refers to a movement in French theology that was prominent just after World War II.

38. Formal causality means that God brings something about by communicating himself.

39. There is also a third factor, the openness of theology to the future, discussed in the last chapter of this book.

40. Neuner and Roos, *op. cit.*, No. 809, 833, and 834.

41. See E. Klinger, ed., *Christentum innerhalb und ausserhalb der Kirche* (Freiburg, 1976), p. 122.

42. H. Küng, 'Anonyme Christen—wozu?', *Orientierung* 39 (1975), p. 215.

43. *Quaestiones disputatae* 73, p. 135.

44. *Op. cit.*, pp. 122–23.

45. *Op. cit.*, pp. 68–69.

46. H. Urs von Balthasar, *Herder-Korrespondenz* 30 (1976), p. 76.

47. See p. 175.

48. *Quaestiones Disputatae* 73, p. 90.

49. Unlike an effective or a formal cause, a final cause is a (partial) cause which brings something about on the basis of an aim. An example of such a final cause is my action if I want to attain something that I have set myself as an aim or end.

50. See also p. 168 ff, the 'important intermediate consideration'.

51. Neuner and Roos, *op. cit.*, No. 78.

200 *Notes*

52. Other factors of course play an important part in the evolution of certain religions, but these are not mentioned here as they are irrelevant to our particular theme.

53. See what is said above.

54. *Ich glaube an Jesus Christus* (*Theologische Meditationen,* 21), ed. H. Küng (Einsiedeln, 1968).

55. Arno Schilson, *Christologie im Präsens* (Freiburg, 1974), p. 89.

56. Denzinger and Schönmetzer, *op. cit.,* 301, 302.

57. Here *a posteriori* faith and *a priori* transcendentality are clearly linked together in an indissoluble circle.

58. This is so despite a history of revelation; see Chapter 7, especially p. 192 ff on the development of dogma and the right of the individual.

59. W. Pannenberg, *Grundzüge der Christologie* (Gütersloh, 2 1969), p. 69.

60. A. Schilson, *op. cit.,* p. 84; see also K. Rahner, *Foundations of Christian Faith, op. cit.,* pp. 295–97.

61. *op. cit.,* p. 85.

62. W. Kasper, *Jesus the Christ* (London & New York, 1977), pp. 120 ff.

63. See above, pp. 170–71.

64. Dogmatic Constitution on Divine Revelation, *Dei Verbum,* 8.

65. *Op. cit.,* 11.

66. *Op. cit.,* 8, 11.

67. The detailed text is in Neuner and Roos, *op. cit.,* No. 468–69.

68. Neuner and Roos, *op. cit.,* No. 469.